A Relentless Hope

A Relentless Hope

*Surviving the Storm
of Teen Depression*

GARY E. NELSON

Cascade Books
A division of Wipf & Stock Publishers
199 West 8th Avenue, Suite 3 · Eugene OR 97401

A RELENTLESS HOPE
Surviving the Storm of Teen Depression

ISBN 13: 978-1-55635-309-3

Cataloging-in-Publication data:

Nelson, Gary E.

A relentless hope : surviving the storm of teen depression / Gary E. Nelson.

xvi + 138 p. ; cm.

Includes bibliography

ISBN 13: 978-1-55635-309-3

1. Pastoral theology. 2. Depression in adolescence. 3. Depression in children. I. Title.

RJ506.D4 N44 2007

*For all the teens who struggle through this terrible storm
and all those who brave the journey with them.*

Contents

Acknowledgments

I OFFER MY deepest thanks to everyone who nurtured, trained, encouraged, and accompanied me on the many roller-coaster rides of life. I know it took the effort of many individuals and communities to see me through this project. Although there are too many to list them all by name, I do need to mention Carey, who helped ground us during the storm and offered suggestions for this manuscript.

Many folks may read this book and recognize a part of the journey we walked together as family, friends, students, teachers, pastors, parishioners, clients, or professional colleagues. Rest assured, my life was blessed by your presence along the way. I hope in the sharing of our journey others will also be blessed.

I especially want to thank Tom, who gave me permission to share his story; Rebekah, who lovingly and courageously rode the coasters with us; Monica, who joined the ride and brought more joy for Tom; and Patti, who gave me the gift of time to write this book, and gives everything it takes to be my soul mate and seatmate on all the coasters.

Introduction

MIRACLES REALLY happen in today's world. This book uses the story of one of those miracles of God's healing as a thread to weave together some of what I've learned in fighting one of the most dangerous monsters of our time—teenage depression. Hopefully what I share in the following pages will benefit other teens and families facing this widespread problem. The story serving as a guide relates the struggle of one of the most courageous young men I have ever known. His name is Thomas Paul Nelson—Tom, for short. He's my son.

Tom's not unique. There are many young folks like him. This book draws from their stories too. All of the teens whose stories are in these pages have been ravaged by illnesses like depression and anxiety, and they've fought to save their lives from the clutches of these killers. Killers? You question? Yes. These are powerful, treacherous killers.

Some studies list suicide as the number-two cause of death of teenagers in our society.[1] Since depression and related illnesses are the driving forces behind most suicides, it's easy to see why I call them potential killers. The number-one killer of teens is the automobile crash, and since alcohol and drugs are often involved, it's possible depression is closer to the top of the "killer-of-teens list" in our country. There's a connection between the alcohol, drugs, car crashes, and depression.

Many teens suffering from depression and related illnesses use alcohol and drugs to block the pain. We call this "self-medicating." Teens killed in car crashes involving alcohol or other drugs may have been self-medicating. Therefore, it's easy to see why depression may be closer to the number-one spot on the "killer-of-teens list."

Depression doesn't always kill. The illness often steals life from teenagers, their families, and friends in many different ways. Relationships are severely damaged or lost. Academic performance is often dramatically stunted. Participation in meaningful activities becomes sporadic. When

---

1. Ontario Consultants on Religious Tolerance, "Facts About Suicide," line 38.

this thief is at work, the enjoyment of life itself is sucked out of the af-flicted teen.

These killers and thieves may claim the top spots on many lists, but amazingly, they are often missed or dismissed by parents and other adults who make comments like, "He's just being an obnoxious teen," or, "It's just that teenage, stuff. I hope we can endure it until she grows out of it." Even worse is, "He's just become a real troublemaker!"

As adults and parents today, we rely too heavily on the questionable explanation that problematic teen behavior is simply a stage of life. We need to be open to the possibility the conduct we write off, as "teens just being teens" is, in fact, an early warning sign of a serious illness, a sickness that could threaten the teen's life.

Teens fighting these illnesses need our understanding, patience, prayers, and help. They don't want to be in our faces, and most aren't really troublemakers. These afflicted teens are being driven by something that makes them act in ways that hurt themselves and those around them. That "something" is what we call depression and related illnesses like anxiety, bipolar disorder, or others.

I am a United Methodist minister who began his career almost thirty years ago as a parish pastor serving churches; later, I returned for more training and education to become a pastoral counselor. For the first twelve years of my career I served local United Methodist churches and spent a lot of time working with the youth of my congregations. We met for study and worship, went on mission trips to give of ourselves for others, spent weekends on retreats, and passed many an hour in playful group-building endeavors.

From parish ministry I returned to graduate school for another degree and additional training. After that I worked the next sixteen years as a pas-toral counselor with an interfaith counseling ministry. Pastoral counselors are trained in theology, various fields of psychology, psychopharmacology, and other social sciences. The blended disciplines help clients find needed healing. I've had people tell me that their pastor or church frowned on their coming to someone like me for help on several occasions. The con-cern was some form of counseling would damage the parishioner's faith. In some cases the parishioners even were told psychology was of the devil.

I can assure you those assumptions are totally unfounded. Pastoral counselors are people of faith who recognize the need for God's miracle of healing to work in many different ways. Over the years of my ministry, there have been several people who courageously walked into my office despite having been told they were entering "the devil's lair;" however, I know there are other tortured souls who never got help because of the religious taboo about counseling imposed by their community of faith.

Not all counselors and other professionals in the mental health field integrate spirituality as part of the helping methodology. They prefer to leave that part of the work for the individual's pastor or spiritual community. These mental health professionals also can provide much needed help to those waging the battle with depression and its allies. Please believe me when I say that these professionals also are not included on the list of " the devil's army." I hope this book will inspire hope, provide helpful information, point the reader toward the path of self-examination, and encourage more people to seek professional mental health care when necessary.

In my pastoral counseling ministry I met teens and their parents in very different situations than those provided by serving as the pastor of a local church. In my pastoral counseling ministry parents would bring their teens to my office for counseling. Most of the time, the family members limped into my office wearing the scars of many emotional (and sometimes physical) battles waged against one another. Unlike my time in parish ministry I had limited contact with teens and their families outside the counseling room.

This book was inspired by my wide-ranging experiences with teens both as a parish pastor and as a pastoral counselor. I'm tackling this killer called depression, and its relatives, from the perspective of one who has worked with teens and their parents in many different situations. I have taught teens, worshipped with teens, played with teens, counseled with teens, and buried teens. In addition to all of that, I am a father. I have encountered these killers of teens in my own home. Depression tried to steal our son from my wife Patti and me.

Today, so much more is known about depression and related illnesses than a generation ago, and yet so much still remains mystery and theory. If professionals in the mental health field are honest, I think many of them will admit it's often difficult to determine if we are dealing with depression alone, or a combination of depression and anxiety, or depression and something else. Are we dealing with several different, distinct illnesses or are we dealing with just one or two illnesses that manifest themselves from one person to another in many different constellations of symptoms? I've heard some experts say that someday we'll probably need new names for these illnesses as we tease apart the symptoms and learn more about the connections between the distinct illnesses we try to name today as depression, anxiety, etc.

Because of this current state of confusion regarding the connection between symptoms and illnesses, I'm going to simplify things for the purposes of this book. For the rest of this book, I'll use the word "depression" to talk about this situation or crisis confronting many teens. In Tom's case, the crisis emerged as a combination of severe depression and severe anxiety.

Depression and anxiety often attack together. For some teens, depression is worse than the anxiety. For other teens, the opposite situation develops, with the anxiety exhibiting the more severe symptoms. Some teens show signs of only one illness, and for yet another group of teens the symptoms early on may mimic depression or anxiety but later manifest as something more like a bipolar disorder or schizophrenia. For the sake of simplicity, I'll just use the word "depression" as an abbreviation to describe the situation or crisis confronting teens and their families.

This is not meant to be a technical book, or the definitive word on depression and related illnesses. This book is intended for teens, parents, pastors, teachers, and other adults who might have personal experience with depression or who might be in a position to offer help for someone else afflicted by the illness. Parts of the book may appeal more to parents than teens and vice versa. Hopefully, teens and parents can share with one another how the story speaks to each one.

For the past couple of years, Tom and I have talked about telling his story so it might help others. Today, Tom is happily married and successful in his chosen career. He is a joy to know. As you can tell from my opening statement, his mother and I are very happy for him. We're also extremely proud of him. Yet, ten years ago the monsters almost got him. His mother, his younger sister (Rebekah), and I almost lost him to the killers that tried to steal Tom's life from him.

In the pages that follow, I'll tell Tom's story and use it as a jumping-off point to talk about the struggles of other teens. Some of Tom's insights as an insider to the struggle are also included. Along the way, I'll offer suggestions for help and hope that will cover a wide range of possibilities, including counseling and medical interventions, spiritual considerations, parental attitudes, and family activities, just to name a few. All of these factors, including help provided by professionals—like counseling, medications, and spiritual guidance—played a very important role in the healing for Tom and our family.

I'm not trying to be dramatic by calling Tom's journey a miracle. As you'll hear later, I am a firm believer we cannot explain everything about life. We cannot explain why a lot of bad things happen to us, those close to us, and strangers in other parts of the world. Yet, even though I cannot explain why Tom was attacked by this treacherous illness called depression, I have to proclaim what I do know. It is a miracle he is alive today. The fact that I cannot explain why the killer attacked in the first place does not negate the fact that a miracle unfolded before my very eyes. I have to name it for what it is. God is at work in our world! Tom's life is evidence of God's amazing healing power.

Tom and I hope you find in the sharing of his miracle the possibilities and hope for your own. God is also working for your healing. *There is help and hope.* "The light shines in the darkness, and the darkness cannot overcome it" (John 1:5).

1

Three Fastballs Down the Middle (of the Hallway)

Looking at Teen Depression from the "Outside"

IT REALLY wasn't what you would call a fight. I'd say it was more of a disagreement between father and son. I don't even remember raised voices. Tom and I were standing at the top of the stairs having some sort of discussion, which ended with him getting less than he wanted. It seemed simple enough. I thought it was settled when we finished talking and Tom walked down the stairs toward his bedroom.

Moments later, three loud "whomps" in quick succession contradicted my assumption. The explosions from the trio of fastballs signaled the beginning of the walk through the valley of the shadow of death that our family was about to begin. The sounds were just as foreign to us as Tom's moods, thoughts, and behaviors would be in the next three years. When did the spaceship land and replace our son with an alien look alike?

The three baseballs Tom hurled through the downstairs hallway wall were the first in a long series of his actions and reactions totally baffling Patti and me. Never had we witnessed such behavior in our home. Never had disagreements or arguments been punctuated by acts of violence. Yet, there they were, the three round holes in the wall, marking the end of a discussion and the beginning of a nightmare.

The three fastballs had found their mark next to the closed door of Tom's room. The door was the gateway to his private sanctuary. Unfortunately, the illness he was fighting soon turned the shelter of his sanctuary into a darkened torture chamber holding him in its clutches and threatening to drain his life force.

Tom was a great baseball player. By the time he was in middle school, he was an accurate pitcher with a seventy-mile an hour fastball. It explained why the holes in the wall were deep and neatly placed in a tight pattern. He was also a home run hitter with an incredibly powerful swing. Tom was good at a lot of things. Folks considered him a pretty well rounded guy who liked his friends, video games, baseball, and whatever else teens do when they "hang out."

Tom's academic record all the way to the end of middle school (sixth through eighth grade) was great. He was pretty self-motivated to complete his work on time and be as successful as possible in his academic endeavors. He made the honor roll many times. At the end of his eighth-grade year he was inducted into the Junior National Honor Society.

He was well liked by his coaches and teachers, and was very well behaved throughout his life. His mother and I enjoyed the compliments paid to him by many other adults. (Well, there was the time he clobbered one of the older women of the church with a snowball.)

I had just started serving as the pastor of a church in Rockport, Massachusetts. The church building had burned to the ground a few months before our arrival, so the congregation was meeting for worship in the basement of the town hall. Tom was five, and feeling his oats. He had just endured another Sunday morning worship service in the basement, and couldn't wait to explode up the basement stairs and jump into the new fallen snow. He raced ahead of the adults to celebrate his freedom.

As one of the older women of the congregation began to ascend the stairs of the exterior basement stairwell, her head slowly appeared above the wall. Tom couldn't resist the temptation. What a target! He plastered the side of her head with some of the newly accumulating ammunition he had expertly formed into a projectile. Fortunately, the woman wasn't injured. The pastor was informed of his son's mischievous behavior. Tom and I made the obligatory trip to her home for an apology. (I still have to admit, it was a huge temptation for a five-year-old, and a great shot as well.) Tom was well liked and appreciated by adults, even the snowball lady.

When Tom was nine years old we moved to northern Virginia where I began my work as a pastoral counselor. Patti and I bought a house with a big empty field across the street, so Tom and Rebekah would have plenty of room to play with friends. As Tom got older, his friends came to our house to hang out or to set up various activities in the field. Many a baseball found its way over the fence into the neighbor's yard during the following sandlot games. They kept the field busy with baseball, football, and softball. When the snow covered the field and the adjacent hill, the sleds came out, and the neighborhood gang assembled for winter fun. The field rarely got a break.

Patti and I also found other ways to support our children's social lives. Our van was often the neighborhood bus for activities like roller-skating and museum trips. When Tom became too old for the traditional birthday parties of his younger years, we'd celebrate his birthday by taking him and a minivan full of his friends to Camden Yards in Baltimore for an Orioles baseball game.

We also had a very active family life. The four of us traveled and played together, enjoying everything from national parks to amusement parks. We went hiking in the woods with our dogs when the weather permitted. When the snow arrived, we hit the slopes with our sleds. When weather trapped us inside, we resorted to board games, hobbies, and movies.

Life was great, so how did we go from enjoying life as a family to wondering if our son would make it through high school, or worse yet, remain alive for years to come? How did we go from laughing and celebrating to crying and cringing in fear? How did Tom wind up being so ugly to his parents and sister? Why did Tom retreat to his darkened bedroom and refuse to leave his bed for days and weeks on end? Why did Tom give up so much that seemed to be going so well for him? Why did Tom refuse to attend school, eventually finishing his education with a GED instead of a diploma? Why did Tom cut himself off from the world and almost bring about the end of his own life? When did the spaceship land and swap our beautiful son for an alien look-alike?

For many, if not most afflicted teens, depression, anxiety, and similar illnesses creep up gradually. Generally, there is not a single significant event the depressed teen can point to as the critical moment when their slide began. Occasionally, Tom would begin the school day by saying he had a stomachache, or that he didn't feel well. When pressed, he really couldn't say what was bothering him.

Gradually, the "I'm sick" days became more frequent. One missed school day began to follow another as Tom finished eighth grade and entered high school. Despite the fact that Patti and I were in frequent contact with his teachers and school counselor, the school's computer started kicking out letters warning he might not pass the year, or that we could be turned over to the truancy department. Fear began to slowly gnaw at our insides like a silent, growing cancer.

Early on in the struggle, Patti and I tried the typical parent responses. "If you're too sick to go to school, then you're too sick to go to your friend's house this evening." We even tried, "If you're too sick to go to school, then you're definitely too sick to play baseball later today." It really didn't seem to matter. No amount of threatening or pushing could change his mind. Tom would just stay in the bed and pull the covers up higher over his head.

It was hard to imagine how Tom could hide under the covers for so long. There were so many interesting and exciting things awaiting him outside the boundaries of his darkened sanctuary. He was leading a very full life when this monstrous illness intensified its attack. Tom wasn't hiding under the covers simply to avoid going to school; he was avoiding life. He wouldn't even come out for his friends.

Tom's buddies would knock at our front door and ask for him. Patti or I would have to tell them that Tom was home, but just didn't want to see them. We could see the puzzled look on their faces as we gave them the news. Tom was their buddy. Why didn't he want to see them? Patti and I began to recognize the same puzzled looks on a lot of faces as we found ourselves trying to explain the mystery of Tom's illness to his teachers, coaches, and friends.

As the depression deepened and more school days were missed, Tom became more and more surly and irritable toward his family. He said ugly things to Patti and me. At times he was pretty hard on his younger sister. Patti and I tried to be observant and keep him from venting his frustrations on Rebekah, but I'm sure we were not always successful.

Along with Tom's surliness came a hair-trigger temper, thus the three baseballs through the wall of the hallway. Tom's anger seemed to come out of nowhere. He could be fairly even tempered one moment and then fly into a rage without a moment's warning. More and more holes began to appear in the walls and ceiling of his room. Tom punched and kicked his painful feelings into the sheetrock that enclosed him in his tomb. The climax came one morning when he almost completely destroyed the door to his room. Something bothered him, so he repeatedly bashed the door with a barbell. The deafening noise almost scared us to death.

After that outburst, we found Tom lying on his bed, sobbing in his pillow. As he lay on his bed with his face buried in his pillow, it finally occurred to Tom what happened with his pummeled door was not a reflection of his true self. Tom knew deep within his soul he didn't want to act that way. Patti and I had figured that out long before the morning of the door incident. We had known for quite awhile that we were not seeing "the real Tom." Unfortunately, it took a while longer for us to help Tom come to that awareness. Tom wanted to believe his anger and moodiness were part of a teenager working out his parental conflicts.

As the door teetered on its hinges, Tom finally realized he was being driven to raging, destructive behavior by some force inside him that wasn't part of his true self. He wasn't acting from his normal personality or feelings. He really didn't want to destroy things around him and damage relationships with people he loved. He finally had to admit to himself that he didn't understand what was happening to him. That was the morning he was finally able to hear me when I explained to him that he was being attacked by the monster we call depression. Finally Tom agreed to let Patti and me get him some outside help. Thank God!

Most of the time Tom was able to handle his ugliness and temper in public. It was mainly reserved for home—lucky us. There were two exceptions I can recall. One night, early in the downward spiral, the four of us went out to dinner and then roller-skating at a local rink. While we were skating, there was some sort of bumping or pushing on the rink that involved Tom and three teenage boys who were strangers to us. The next thing I knew, Tom and the three young men were doing the teen posturing dance as though a fight was about to break out. I was shocked! I had never seen Tom handle himself like that. He was angry and ready to fight.

The other incident involving "public ugliness" happened several months later. A baseball coach was laying into Tom and giving him some pretty harsh criticism. Tom snapped, knocked over the water cooler and stormed out of the dugout. His temper flared instantly. He stormed out of the dugout and off the team.

As the strange and sometimes overwhelming feelings mounted, Tom became more and more isolated from the rest of his world. It was harder for him to do even the things he used to enjoy. His friends couldn't get him to go out with them. He even pulled away from baseball. For a while, his mother, sister, and I were his only companions. Often it took every sort of urging, persuading, pushing, and dragging we could muster just to get him to leave the house and do something fun with us.

The real problem was that nothing was "fun" anymore. Tom felt more numbed than anything. In his mind, there was no reason to bother trying to do anything that might be fun. Nothing he could imagine could make him feel any better or different than numb. He was at the place of despair. The monster really had its hold on him.

The "down side" of the depression was also hidden from the public. When Tom was out and about, no one could tell there was anything wrong. He looked and acted pretty "normal" for a teenager. He wore brightly colored sports jerseys emblazoned with his favorite teams' logos. He interacted with his friends in a healthy manner. Adults found him to be thoughtful, friendly, and helpful.

When Tom entered high school, he began to miss more and more days of school. Eventually, Patti and I went to the school for a team meeting with all of his teachers. His teachers said, "We don't understand why we're all sitting here in this conference. When Tom is in school, he's a delight to be around. His classmates love him. We wish we had thirty more students just like him. When he gets up in front of the class to make a presentation, his content is excellent, and his delivery is incredibly entertaining. Last week Tom was doing a report about baseball and had the whole class doing 'the wave' like they were at the stadium."

Patti and I responded, "We know the Tom you're describing. He's great. But here's the other part you don't see. When Tom is not in school, he's home lying on his bed in a dark room. He's not 'skipping' school so he can do something else instead of schoolwork. He won't come out of his room for anyone or anything." The teachers and school staff in the conference shook their heads in amazement. It just didn't seem as though the two pictures were describing the same teen. How could the picture painted by the school staff be so bright and promising, while the picture presented by Patti and me was so dark and troubling? Sadly, both pictures really were describing the same troubled youth.

Part of the difficulty in fighting teenage depression is being able to identify it as it sneaks up on the teen. There is no one typical pattern that depression follows. There are signs that may hint at the presence of depression or a related illness, but the signs do not always coalesce into the same picture. Some teens may live a fairly normal public life and hide a private hell. Others may publicly display the wounds inflicted by the monster in their appearance and their actions. The truth is, it can be very difficult for the average person to spot a teen who is suffering from depression or one of its relatives. At times, it's even difficult for professionals to spot these terrible maladies. That's why we need more public discussion and education around depression and its related illnesses.

The subtlety and complexity of depression can make it difficult to spot. However, there are other reasons depression in teens can continue without being identified. Sometimes the untreated afflictions of the parents blind them to the struggles of their child. Not long ago I preached a sermon at a church and used part of Tom's story as an example. A few days later I received a thank-you card from a young mother in her midthirties.

The young woman explained she had suffered tremendously from depression only a year before. Finally she went for professional help. In her words, "I had my 'high' times but mostly I was at an even low. Last year though I could no longer function and bring myself out of it. I saw my doctor and he put me on Zoloft (an antidepressant medication) and I can now look at every day as a gift instead of torment. Why my parents never saw the tears I cried every day I'll never know. We have a terrible lineage of mental illness and addictions." This young woman answered her own question. Her parents probably couldn't see her struggles because of their own issues. If we want to help our children, we had better face our own demons first. We'll get back to that later in this story.

Sometimes I've described the way people fighting depression appear to others by comparing depressed people to plates of food at a potluck lunch after church. The depressed person is the "filled plate," and the various foods on the table are the symptoms of depression. If I send ten people through the potluck line and tell them to fill their plates, all of them will finish with plates that look very different.

Some of the church members will load up on meat and potatoes and some will hit the green vegetables heavier. Others will get just few enough selections of healthier food to avoid being embarrassed by the mountain of desserts heaped upon their plates and dangling from the sides. (You can't hide. I've seen your plates!) The ten hungry parishioners all went to the same potluck table, yet their plates look very, very different. Ten people ("filled plates") may all be depressed, but their particular collection of symptoms (foods on the table and their plates) may wind up making them look quite different from one another.

Before "leaving the table," I'll add a little more about some of those "food items" at the potluck. In other words, let me mention some of the more typical symptoms of depression and anxiety. It's hard to tell sometimes if one of the symptoms is more from depression or anxiety, since the two illnesses frequently occur in the same individual.

I've already mentioned the irritability and moodiness plaguing Tom. These symptoms are often intensified by an irregularity and disruption in sleep patterns. As Tom's illness progressed, his sleep pattern became very chaotic. As Patti and I were winding down for the night, we could see Tom was winding up. This made it very difficult for him to fall asleep and stay asleep. Many studies have shown that sleep disruption is a major issue accompanying depression in teens and adults.

Other symptoms include difficulty concentrating, getting stuck on certain thoughts, isolating from friends and family, lack of energy, change in appetite, weight loss or gain, decline in academic grades, lack of interest in normal pleasurable activities, experimentation with drugs or alcohol, interest in high-risk activities, outbursts of crying, sadness, acts of self-mutilation, or even a sense of just feeling "stuck" or "numb." Some teens may have lots of symptoms from the list while others may exhibit only a few. The intensity of each symptom might also vary from teen to teen.

When you look at the list, you can probably say, "Doesn't everyone experience many or even most of those feelings from time to time?" Yes, you're right. As a matter of fact, one of the problems we have today in helping people understand more about depression is that we use the same word, "depression," to describe two different things. We use the same word to describe the typical feeling that all of us experience from time to time as well as the medical illness that we're discussing in this book. This dual use of the same word makes it very confusing for the depressed teen as well as those around them trying to help.

Everyone feels depressed now and then. It's a typical human feeling. Depression might accompany the death of a loved one or some other significant loss. A major life transition like a move to a new city or going off to college might also give rise to this more typical kind of depression. Sometimes we just feel "blue" for no apparent reason. These experiences of feeling depressed are short lived, generally lasting for only a few days. Then we're able put it away and go on. We feel better, more like our old selves again. We say we were a little depressed, but we got over it. That's not what Tom and others like him experienced.

The kind of depression Tom fought is often known as "clinical depression." It generally lasts for weeks, months, even years, and is much more intense. Generally, the quality of life is significantly diminished for its victims. There are a multitude of symptoms and difficulties associated with this medical illness. It is really important to understand this difference between the two uses of "depression" if we are to be of help to those who are clinically depressed.

Often people try to help someone fighting clinical depression with suggestions like, "Why don't you think positive thoughts?" Or, "Give your worries to God," just to name a few. These are well-meaning people. Probably, they successfully tried the same suggestions when they felt down or depressed. The problem is, the would-be helper thinks the clinically depressed person suffers from the same depression the helper experienced. If the two are experiencing the same ailment, it makes sense to offer suggestions that worked for the concerned helper. However, the problems afflicting the two are not the same. They may look similar on the outside, but the similarity ends there.

The clinical depression doesn't generally respond as easily to simple encouragement. In this situation where a helper is offering advice that worked for them, both the helper and the depressed person can walk away from the encounter feeling more frustrated. The helper feels frustrated because it seems to them that the depressed person just isn't trying hard enough, isn't doing it the right way, or simply doesn't want their help. After all, the same suggestions have worked for the helper when they felt depressed (but not clinically depressed). The helper might even leave thinking that the depressed person just wants to be depressed. "Maybe they like the attention it gets them," the helper might wonder.

The clinically depressed person can also leave the encounter feeling more frustrated. They often feel even more unknown by the helper, and thus more and more isolated. "Don't they think I've tried those things, already?" the depressed one thinks about the helper. "Don't they know how much I really want to get rid of this, how much I'd love for God to simply take it away? Why are they offering such lame advice?" When you really stop and think about it, a lot of the statements well-meaning helpers make to depressed persons can seem pretty lame.

The fact is, people can say some pretty lame, even irrational and unhelpful things when they feel helpless. I think the worst example I ever heard was at the funeral of a child. I was standing near the parents when I overheard a well-meaning friend say, "God must have needed your child more than you. That must be why God has taken them back."

I know the friend felt extremely helpless in the face of such a tragic loss and only wanted to comfort the parents. Unfortunately, the statement of support they uttered didn't accomplish their desired end. Instead, they stumbled over their helplessness and said something that wasn't very help-ful. We have to face our own helplessness in difficult situations and be very careful that it doesn't push us to do or say things that are not as helpful as we intend. I'll say more about the dangers of this helplessness in the fight against depression later in this book.

The same misunderstanding about "everyday" depression and clini-cal depression surrounds anxiety and clinical anxiety. We use the word "anxiety" to describe two different experiences. Everyone feels anxious from time to time. There's even a more positive use of the word "anxiety." For example, we can feel anxious for Christmas to arrive and usher in the joyous celebrations with family and friends. However, we might also feel anxious in a more negative way about the arrival of the holiday if we haven't finished our shopping or baked all the cookies. The use of the same word gets confusing.

Most students feel anxious when they know they are facing a test in school. As a matter of fact, a little anxiety can be helpful. It's a natural warning that awakens us physically and mentally. A little of the right kind of anxiety acts as a wake-up call and alerts us to the fact that something important may be about to happen. Maybe it will encourage us to study harder for the upcoming test.

Too much anxiety becomes destructive. One student might feel much more anxiety than is necessary for a simple wake-up call. She or he might feel thoughts racing and become too distracted to study for the test. They try to study, but nothing gets through. They feel so anxious that they can't focus on what they're trying to study or can't retain the material they're trying to commit to memory. Another student might be able to study but feel so anxious sitting down to begin the test that their mind races or goes blank. The anxious student knew the material ten minutes earlier when they were standing in the hallway outside the testing room. Star-ing at the page in front of them, they panic and fail to recall the needed information.

We would call this experience of too much anxiety "clinical anxiety." This kind of anxiety doesn't help. It gets in the way. It hurts. Not everyone feels this kind of anxiety. Yet when people talk with one another about feeling anxious, they may not realize they could be talking about two dif-ferent experiences. One experience of anxiety is manageable and maybe even helpful. The other encounter with anxiety is incredibly destructive.

At some point you're probably wondering, "Where does all this come from? How does a teen 'get' clinical depression or one of its relatives like anxiety?" I might as well speak to that now. Like many other things about depression, a lot is known and a lot can only be surmised from the evidence available. I think it's safe to say a lot of professionals would conclude that depression emerges from some interaction of nature and nurture. In other words, we know there are environmental events that can trigger bouts of depression and anxiety, but something else about the natural, more genetically determined make-up of the person must also be involved.

These environmental triggers can include some tragic loss, a family crisis, a severe illness, or even a reaction to particular drugs. However, there is something more than environmental events involved for many people in the onset of these illnesses. As I've said earlier, there are many depressed persons who can't relate their illness to any single event. For some, it just seems like it's been with them most of their lives.

I worked with an organization called the Center for Pastoral Counseling of Virginia. The Center has offices in churches all around the northern Virginia and Washington, D.C., metropolitan area. After the tragic events of September 11, 2001, we had a lot of people who came to our offices suffering from episodes of depression and anxiety. Our colleagues working in other counseling centers had similar experiences. Many of the folks who sought counseling worked in or near the Pentagon on September 11.

Now, did the airplane crashing into the Pentagon cause most of those people, who showed up for help around the same time, to feel depressed and anxious? Was the plane crash the environmental trigger that caused the depression and anxiety? The answer is, of course, "yes." Too many people with stories connected to the plane crash showed up for help at the same time for it to have been mere coincidence.

The environmental event traumatized a lot of people at the same time. However, if the airplane crash "caused" the depression and anxiety, why didn't all the survivors of the crash experience it? Why didn't all the survivors become depressed or anxious? There must have been something else that contributed to certain people becoming depressed and anxious while others escaped the illnesses. That "something else" is what is known as genetic predisposition. In other words, the tendency to suffer from depression is genetic. It's passed on through families like eye color and other attributes.

Picture this. I'm sitting in my counseling office with a depressed teen and their parent or parents. We talk for a while, and I explain to all of them that the teen is fighting a medical illness known as depression. At some point it is inevitable that one of the people in the room will ask, "Okay, so where did it come from?" I love it. They've fallen into my trap. I get to watch it happen again. Here goes. With the straightest, most wise face I can muster without laughing because I know what's about to happen, I look squarely at the teen and say, "I'm afraid you have clinical depression because your parents had sex."

For a moment, it's so quiet in the room you can hear the fat sizzle on a fast food fry. Then slowly you start to see the ends of the teen's lips begin to curl gently upward. Next, the lips tear open their mouth that has been frozen in a tortured frown for so long, and a full grin bursts forth, eventually allowing a long imprisoned chorus of laughter to escape.

The parents are always caught off guard and even initially embarrassed. Yet, when they see that grin start to appear on their teen's face, they can't resist the urge to join in the laughter. For a moment, the parents feel reconnected with their teen. What a sacred moment it is for the family to share together! What a sacred privilege it is for me to be allowed to share that moment with them!

In case I don't say it enough later, you can't get enough laughter and humor! Just be careful. Remember that when people are depressed, they may not feel the "fun" as much. Humor can help. Just be careful it doesn't frustrate the depressed teen if they can't feel it. Timing is everything.

My digression is meant to say that in most cases I've seen, it's become pretty clear that depression runs in the family. Sometimes the teen and parents can identify the connections immediately and tell me about others in the family tree who have suffered from depression. One or both parents might have been treated for depression (or should have been). Other times it takes more education about the illnesses before the family members in my office can identify relatives in their extended family who might have fought depression.

All too often the depression is hidden behind something like alcoholism or some other more common addition. In many cases, when counselors get someone to quit using alcohol or other drugs, we find they have been using them to self-medicate for some illness like depression. Often I've gotten a negative response from a person when I've asked them if there is a history of depression in their family. Then, when I follow it by asking about a history of alcoholism, they respond with, "Oh sure, there was Grandpa Bob, and Aunt Martha, and cousin Joe."

The depression was hidden in the family behind the alcoholism. The problems caused by the depression and alcoholism probably were not so hidden. Lots of conflict, tragedy, and pain may have occurred in the family and been attributed to alcoholism. Yet, without proper diagnosis and treatment, the depression wreaked havoc while the individual continued to self-medicate with the alcohol.

Historically, depression and its relatives like anxiety have been kept pretty secret in most discussions among family members. It's often difficult to make some of the connections and see the family history of the illness. Sometimes it's not so hard. When Tom began to suffer, I knew of some connections in our family tree but was surprised by others. I knew that I had lived with my share of anxiety growing up. Most of the time, I had been able to fight through it.

Like Tom, I was also a good student in school. Being a good student comes with blessings and curses. The blessings are the more obvious rewards that result from achieving good grades. The curse is the extra intensity and pressure that the good student experiences, not just from parents and teachers, but peers as well. Unfortunately, there's a sort of hierarchy of "good" and "bad" students that gets created in many schools. There's pressure for students on both ends of the hierarchy. One day in fourth grade I wasn't feeling well and failed a math test. By the time I made it to the playground for recess, it seemed the entire school knew that I had failed the test. Several of the children from other classes were taunting me with their jeers.

I have a very clear picture of leaving for school one morning somewhere close to the same time as the failed test. I must have been anxious about another test I was having that day. On this particular morning as I left for school, my mother noticed my heightened anxiety. As I walked out the door she said, "Just ask God to help you do your best today." What a simple but powerful declaration! What an enormous sense of relief for an anxious person! What a profound proclamation of a parent's and God's grace! I've repeated that coaching to myself on many occasions. It came back to me in an especially helpful way when I found myself in the midst of Tom's struggles.

Tom's anxiety and depression were overwhelming and paralyzing. It wasn't that I was stronger than he, so I could fight the feelings and keep them from overwhelming me. No, Tom is very strong and courageous. He simply had more of the depression and anxiety to fight. He was a very good student. Patti and I had been careful not to pressure him unduly about getting good grades. We tried our best to protect him from too much pressure around grades and performance in school. Given his strength of character and our lack of pressure, we couldn't figure out why he seemed so overwhelmed by school. Yet, I also knew from my own experience that these things like depression and anxiety could come out of nowhere, gain momentum, and take on a life all of their own.

I never knew the ravages of depression like Tom, and only once did I experience such overwhelming anxiety that it left its mark on me. I was a senior in high school. I was a very good musician who had performed in front of thousands of people. I had spoken publicly and acted in plays. My debate partner and I had won several championships prior to the event I'm about to describe. Forgive me if it seems I'm "bragging." It always bothers me to have to recount these kinds of accomplishments. I'm merely trying to set the stage for what I'm about to describe. I want you to understand how much the anxiety that paralyzed me just came out of the blue. Given my prior successes, logic would never have predicted this next experience I'm about to relate.

When I was a senior, my high-school speech teacher decided that I would give the "address" at the Thanksgiving assembly in our school. We had those kinds of assemblies in the "dark ages" of long ago. The choir sang and the orchestra played. I walked up on the stage in the auditorium and approached the podium to address about half the student body of three thousand. We had to have two assemblies because the whole student body was too big to fit in the auditorium at one time.

As I started to read my speech, I realized that the words on the page were blurring. It was a very strange experience. I was having a conversation in my head with myself at the same time I was trying to deliver the speech. "What's going on," I wondered as I struggled to get the message across. "This is feeling very weird." The teachers in the auditorium thought I was drunk as a skunk, because my tongue got thick as molasses and my speech began to slur. Eventually the lights went dim for me, I passed out cold, and the assistant principal dragged me off the stage. The next thing I knew I was on the cot in the nurse's station at the school.

An hour later I got up in front of the second half of the student body and gave the speech with no problems. However, the anxiety attack left its mark. To this day, I still have no idea what caused that initial anxiety attack. Maybe I had a flu bug working on me. Maybe I was aware that my new girlfriend was sitting in the student body and would hear my speech. I'll never know. That kind of anxiety attack had never happened to me before, but the anxious pathway it left in my brain seemed to take on a life of its own. The anxious pathway blazed in my brain got progressively stronger over time.

From that point onward, any effort on my part to speak in public was met with tremendous anxiety. As I approached the appointed time to step before an audience, my insides would churn and my knees would shake. Sometimes my knees would shake so hard I would have to hold on to the podium or pulpit to keep from falling. Oh yeah, remember? I was called by God to be a pastor. That meant I had to face a congregation every Sunday.

I tried everything I could think of to stop the anxiety—prayer, meditation, public speaking techniques. I even learned to fake a cough so I could stop talking long enough to catch my breath. With time in front of the same congregation the symptoms would ease, but never stop. It was only later that I discovered the relief I had needed for many years. I'll tell you about that in a later chapter.

Remember how I said these things like depression and anxiety can hide? Here's the kicker to this story. I'm known as a very good preacher. No one could ever tell how extremely anxious I was feeling as I preached or gave a talk. No one knew there were times I could barely talk or stand because I felt so anxious!

I knew about anxiety. I knew how it had hampered me, but I didn't know the more devastating aspects of anxiety and depression that Tom fought. I knew that anxiety and depression ran in both sides of our family and that Tom had inherited some of it from me. I was still surprised to find some of the other connections as Patti and I shared his journey with our families.

Tom was the first grandchild on both sides of our extended families. He is named for both his grandfathers. He gets the "Tom" from my father, with whom he shared and still shares a very special bond. My father was a very successful traveling salesman for many years until his retirement. Up until Tom was about five, we lived on one of my father's weekly routes.

As soon as Tom was old enough, Grandpa would stop by our house and take Tom home with him and Nanny for the night, then deliver him back to Patti and me the next day. I wondered what the long-term effects might be of Tom's listening to endless repeats of Boxcar Willie's version of "Mule Train" on his grandpa's car stereo as they traveled back and forth. Apparently the only result was to help cement the bond between grandpa and grandson.

As Tom slipped into the depression, I wondered how in the world I would explain it to my father. I wasn't sure he would quite understand. It didn't seem to me that this sort of thing was part of his world. All I ever knew was that he seemed to get things done and would push me to do the same when necessary. Tom was in a state where pushing was not the answer. I was afraid my father would think I was parenting the wrong way.

One day the time arrived for me to try to explain to my parents what was happening to Tom. Up until that point Patti and I had kept a lot of it to ourselves. When I finished describing what Tom was going through, my father simply said, "You know, I'll bet that was some of what I was going through when I would pull up to a customer's office and just feel like I couldn't even get out of my car, get my briefcase, and go in to make the call."

At that moment I felt the relief wash my fear away. My father (and mother) understood. It would be okay. They have continued to be some of Tom's greatest supporters. This depression stuff runs in families. Sometimes you see it, sometimes you don't. The more it gets talked about, the better things feel for everyone.

Depression is another one of the illnesses where early detection and intervention are critical. Depression can occur in young teens, preteens, and even children. I know such statements can make it seem that professionals like myself are trying to see depression everywhere we look. That's really not the case. The more we have worked with depressed people, the more aware we have become of the illness's early roots for many people.

I entered clinical training as a pastoral counselor when Tom was about five years old. By the time I made it through five years of training and had amassed some field experience, I had already missed what were probably early signs of things to come in Tom's life. Tom's early symptoms were more clustered around the anxiety that was later to become so powerful with the depression. When Patti and I were parenting Tom through his early years we mistakenly identified early experiences of Tom's anxiety as "shyness." As Patti and I later were plunged into Tom's teenage nightmare, we were able to look back and identify events and behaviors that were probably early signs of his anxiety and depression.

I recall what I now term "the French fry affair." When Tom was about five, we were eating at his favorite restaurant, McDonald's. Tom finished his French fries and asked for more. I said, "Sure, you can have more fries," and reached in my wallet for the money. We were sitting at a table that probably was only about ten feet from the serving counter, with nothing in between the serving counter and our table. I glanced at the counter and saw that no one was in line. I thought to myself, "I'll bet Tom would love to take the money to the counter and ask for his own fries." He was at that age where most children like to do "grownup" things for themselves.

I handed Tom the dollar and said, "Here, you can be a big boy and go get the fries yourself." Instead of jumping for the dollar and racing to the counter, Tom ducked his head and said, "I don't want them." Surprised, I prodded just a bit, then went and got him the French fries. He ate every last one of them.

Tom really wanted the fries, but the ten feet to the counter might as well have been the Grand Canyon. Crossing that space and asking for the fries was just too emotionally overwhelming. At the time, Patti and I just figured he was too shy to get his own fries. (When his younger sister was about the same age, she took the money and made a dash for the counter.) As we looked back on the event from Tom's teen years, we realized the "French fry affair" was probably an early encounter with Tom's anxiety.

Another example of early signs was repeated on several occasions. These signs appeared when Tom was probably about five or six, or maybe even a little older. If Tom misbehaved, we would send him to his room for time out. Often, the misbehavior occurred around an incident similar to the later "fastballs-down-the-hallway affair." If Tom didn't get what he wanted, he would get upset and respond inappropriately. Then we'd send him to his room. However, what we began to notice was that instead of sitting on his bed and cooling off, Tom became more and more upset.

At first Patti and I thought that he was just trying to manipulate us by crying louder and louder. So, like most parents, we ignored the cries and stood our ground. Then we began to notice that Tom was escalating to a point of being emotionally out of control. It was as though he was in a state of panic. He was in some "state," whatever you wanted to call it.

Patti and I discovered that instead of letting Tom cry it out alone, we needed to sit with him and help him calm down. We didn't necessarily give in to his demands, but we did have to do some creative negotiating to get him to calm down and avoid the panic state. It was tricky to get him calm, and still avoid his learning to use the incident as a way to manipulate us.

It became evident that although the incident may have begun with Tom getting angry and upset because he didn't get his way, it changed into something else quite rapidly. Tom entered what I was later to label "an altered state." He wasn't trying to rev himself up and get to the agitated state. His emotions flooded him and drove him there. Once there, he was not the same rational child with whom we could normally communicate and negotiate.

We learned that the only thing to do in those situations was to help him get out of that altered state. Nothing could be accomplished while he was there. Emotionally pushing and threatening only made it worse. This was a foreshadowing of the "altered states" of anger and rage that were to come as a teen. I will say more about these "altered states" later. For now, allow me to offer one other example of a young child I recently encountered in a store, who was suffering from a similar experience of emotional flooding and was driven to an altered state.

Patti and I were looking for something on a shelf in a large department store. Suddenly I heard a child crying a few aisles over. I think it's safe to say the child was "screaming bloody murder." I could tell from the sound that it was a very young child, but something else also occurred to me. When I heard the child, I immediately thought that the cry sounded like panic.

A few moments later, the family rounded the aisle with the child. There were the mom and dad, patiently trying to comfort what looked to be about a three-year-old boy in the shopping cart. His older sister was walking beside them. The parents weren't yelling and screaming at the child in the cart. They weren't saying threatening things to him. The parents weren't being mean to him. Yet the look on the child's face was sheer panic. The whole affair probably started with something like, "No, you can't have the red balloon," and quickly progressed to an altered state of panic for the child. These things like anxiety and depression can sometimes begin at an early age and go unrecognized for years.

You can see from my accounts that these illnesses might be hard to identify. They don't necessarily look the same or begin at the same time. Even though they can occur very early for some, most of the teens I've counseled would tell you they began to feel different somewhere around the end of middle school (eighth grade).

Generally, when you meet a teen who might be fighting depression, they can't tell you immediately when it started. Part of that is because they don't realize anything is going on as the depression is starting to do its work. Sounds strange, doesn't it. Here's what I mean. The teen may not like how they begin to feel. They may feel hurt, perplexed, numb, etc. but they assume that the chaotic jumble of intense feelings storming inside of them is just part of being who they are—a teenager. This is their first time through a lot of the complex feelings that are part of life for all of us. Depressed teens that are feeling more intensity than other teens assume everyone feels the same as they feel, and just handles it differently, or better.

Maybe the teen does realize that their feelings are not the same as those experienced by most teens. If that's the case, they may assume the "different part" of their feelings and behaviors comes from what they think is their "faulty" personality. It's just them. It's just who they are. It's how God made them. They can't change it. They (and others) will just have to learn to live with this faulty personality. They continue to build their identity and life on this false assumption, and more and more pain follows close behind.

It takes a lot of educating for depressed teens to be able to sort out what is a more "typical" feeling, and what is really a symptom of their illness. They need to understand that everyone feels both similar to and different from others. However, the teen has to learn that some of the "difference" they are feeling is coming from a medical condition. There are some feelings and an intensity of most feelings that may be more unique to their medical condition. The depression is giving them something more to handle than most other teens encounter.

Partly because the afflicted teen thinks what they're feeling is "normal," and partly because it just hurts, they begin to act in ways that may complicate their lives. They may hold themselves together in public yet let out all of their ugly feelings and frustrations at home. They may isolate from others. They may become very reactive with adults and take on the persona of "the trouble maker." They might begin to hang out with "the wrong crowd." The depressed teen might become withdrawn and isolated. They might engage in self-destructive behaviors like self-mutilation or eating disorders. The depressed teen might learn to "self-medicate" with alcohol and drugs. They might decide to corner the market on black clothes and dye their hair sixty million different beautiful shades of rain-bow colors. (That's not to say that every teen that likes black clothes and brightly colored hair is depressed). A group of depressed teens may look and act somewhat differently from each other but still be suffering from similar illnesses. Remember the potluck lunch example and all the different plates.

Depression can strike about the same time in life that all teens are struggling with the issue of identity. All young teens are asking questions like, "Who am I like? What makes me feel good about myself? Who do I want to hang out with? What am I good at? What is the 'uniform' for the group I like to be with? Who understands me? What is fun and who is doing it? Where do I belong?" If depression strikes during this time, it may greatly influence the identity that begins to form for the teen.

It's a sad picture when a depressed teen comes to my office for counseling. Seldom does the teen ask for help and seek counseling. They're usually sitting across from me because their parents forced them to see a counselor. Generally, neither the teen nor their parents enter with any idea that some medical illness might be afflicting the teen. Most of the time the family is in my office because the parents are very frustrated with the teen. Why the parents are frustrated can be very different from one family to another.

Sometimes the parents are frustrated because the teen has been in trouble and doesn't seem to care much about changing their self-destructive behavior. The teen just wants everyone to leave them alone. Usually in these cases the teen enters with that look on their face that says, "Everyone else tells me I'm an obnoxious screw-up. How long will it take you to say it? Go ahead say it, so I can get angry and storm out of here. I know this is a waste!" In reality their parents may or may not be saying the teen is an obnoxious screw-up; however, for the teen, it sure feels like that's what everyone is saying.

Actually, that's one of depression's evil tricks. The depression not only changes how we feel, it changes how we think and perceive. (More about that later.) If the parents really are saying some variation of, "You're an obnoxious screw-up," it only makes matters worse. By saying those sorts of things, the parents are helping to create a distorted self-image for the teen and pushing them to live into that exaggerated image.

Sometimes the parents are frustrated because they know something is going on for their son or daughter, but they just can't get their teen to tell them what's wrong. Maybe the teen has been in trouble, but maybe not. Possibly grades have dropped, or more conflicts have emerged with their friends. The parents can tell something is wrong, so they ask, "What's wrong?" The teen replies, "Nothing," or "I don't know." The teen's response frustrates the parents even more. The parents know something is wrong, but the teen is making them feel very helpless and very frustrated. Eventually, the parents may seek professional help for the teen. That's when it becomes the counselor's job to educate the parents and teen about the monster called depression that has been living with the teen and parents.

"If depression can look so different, how are parents to know if their teen is fighting this monster and needs some kind of help?" That's a good question. Every teen encounters difficult struggles, emotionally charged relationships, disappointments, and loss. I'll talk about more of the symptoms of depression and anxiety in the next chapter as we look at what it's like from the inside of the depressed teen. Here, let me say that it's important for parents to remember a simple point that I truly, truly believe. Teens are just like the rest of us. They want to succeed, they don't want to hurt others and themselves, and they really don't want to get in trouble. They may make mistakes that sometimes cause them trouble, but they don't really want to be in trouble or be told that they are trouble.

If you tell a teen that not doing their homework will get them failing grades and they'll have to repeat the class, most teens will do their homework (even if it is begrudgingly). They don't want to fail, and so they make decisions that will promote their success. They do their homework. However, depressed teens want to succeed like everyone else but may feel overwhelmed by the homework, put it off, and eventually fail to complete it. They know they might fail, but facing that distant, eventual consequence seems far easier than living with the feelings of being so overwhelmed in the moment.

Think about that for just a minute. If you've never felt that kind of depression, it may be very difficult to comprehend how someone can fail to do something like homework, knowing that their failure will bring really bad consequences. As a parent or other adult trying to help a depressed teen you have to learn to ask yourself, "What must the teen facing a pile of homework feel in the moment that is so powerful that it pushes them to make the irrational decision? What force is so strong that it pushes the depressed teen to leave the homework uncompleted and lie about their efforts to their parents, knowing all along that their lies will be exposed when semester reports are sent home by the teachers?" Have you ever stopped to think about it that way?

In other words, when parents see their teens making irrational decisions about important areas of their young lives, the parents should be cautious and begin to wonder if something might be behind that irrational process. When teens make decisions that "don't make sense," that sort of decision-making process in and of itself may be an indicator that the monster we call depression is at the door. I don't believe teens want to be "stuck." I don't believe they want to fail. I don't believe teens want to say and do things that hurt their family and others. I don't believe teens want to hurt themselves. Yet, depressed teens do get stuck, they do fail, and they do hurt others and themselves. That's when depressed teens and their families need outside help from professionals. The monster we call depression may be knocking at the door.

2

"All My Bones Are Out of Joint"
(Psalm 22:14)

Looking at Teen Depression
from the "Inside"

ONE DAY Patti and I were straightening Tom's room while he was away. Now lest you think we were searching the room and going through his things, let me explain. I've had parents ask me if they should periodically search their children's rooms or backpacks just to keep tabs on them. Generally, my answer is, "No." Privacy is important to all of us. If your teen seems to be leading a fairly healthy life, then grant them their privacy.

Teens experiment with a lot of ideas and feelings as they form their own set of opinions and values. Trust your child unless they begin to give you really good reason not to, and even then, cross the line into the invasion of their privacy very carefully and with great restraint. If safety and health are at risk, the rule of privacy may have to be bent, but cautiously, and openly.

That's basically where Patti and I found ourselves. We had always trusted Tom to the max, but then he began to lie to us about homework and school projects. It just wasn't like him to lie to us. Tom was missing a lot of school. He was becoming more and more belligerent. We were fairly certain he wasn't into anything like drugs or alcohol, but the radical changes in his behavior even made us wonder about that. He couldn't or wouldn't tell us that anything was wrong in his life. We searched our minds, but we didn't search his room, clothes, or backpack. We just used cleaning his room as an excuse to poke around.

If your teen has given you hard evidence to think that he or she might be into destructive behaviors like drug use, then searching is not out of the question, in my opinion. The teen would need to know that they have broken the covenant of safety for the home and its other occupants, so privacy may be sacrificed until trust can be rebuilt. In other words, don't be sneaky about searching. Let the teen know that trust has been severely violated and therefore their room or belongings might be checked. Safety trumps privacy.

The same would hold if a teen has hurt or seriously talked about hurting themselves in other ways. For example, if a teen has gone behind their locked bedroom door and taken an overdose of pills, the bedroom door might have to stay open when the teen is alone in their room until trust could be regained. If a teen has made unhealthy contacts on the computer in their bedroom, the computer might have to be moved to a "public" location in the house until trust can be reestablished. All this said, parents should show great restraint before invading the privacy of their teens.

We didn't search Tom's things, but we periodically straightened his disheveled room (more like disaster zone), because he was so overwhelmed by it. Sometimes Patti and I helped him straighten his room, and sometimes we straightened it by ourselves while he was away. I will admit we used this as an opportunity to find any clues that might help us help him. He knew we might help straighten his room or change his bedclothes, so I figured things we found lying around were fair game. It was during one of those "straightening sweeps" when he was away that I found the paper on the floor.

The paper was folded, so I thought at first it might be a note to a friend. Maybe it would provide a clue to our predicament. The folded paper turned out to be part of an essay Tom had written for health class. It didn't help us in terms of providing an answer for why Tom was feeling and acting in the strange new ways. However, Tom's writing on the paper did provide me with one of the most graphic pictures of depression that I have ever encountered. I'm not sure what prompted the writing, but simply put, Tom said that feeling depressed was like, "being beaten from the inside."

Take a moment and let that sink in. Recall a picture you've seen of a person who has been severely beaten. Sometimes the bruising and swelling are so bad that the victim's features are grotesquely contorted. The bruises, cuts, and scrapes on the outside scream the agony the beaten soul must suffer deep from within. Every bone in their body aches, every muscle throbs. Maybe it even hurts to be touched. You can't imagine how the beaten person must feel, and shudder at the thought of even trying to consider it. The picture even may make you want to turn away. The sight is just too awful.

Now take that picture and turn it inside out. Imagine you're sitting next to someone who looks exactly like that beaten person turned inside out. On the inside they bear all the same marks and trauma, but somehow manage to conceal it from you. That's how, Tom described, it felt to be depressed. It's like "being beaten from the inside." It's sounds so awful that I'm not sure I want to even attempt to imagine how that must feel.

One of the best descriptions of depression I have found comes from the Old Testament of the Bible. When people look to the Psalms, I think they tend to gravitate towards the passages they feel are more uplifting, like psalms of joy, praise, and thanksgiving. Often we skip over the difficult accounts of hardship and suffering that are also a testimony of faith and hope, yet in a slightly different way.

Frequently I have asked people suffering from depression to read Psalm 22. "My God, my God, why have you abandoned me? I have cried desperately for help but still it does not come" (verse 1). There's the isolation of depression that people describe. Do you hear it? What about the lack of self-esteem and confidence that accompanies depression? Verse 6 speaks to that. "But I am no longer a man; I am a worm, despised and scorned by everyone! All who see me make fun of me and shake their heads." You can't feel much lower than a worm.

Then there's the sense of sheer hurt, lethargy, and numbness depression brings that is so difficult to describe, what Tom put in such a succinct word picture with his "beaten from the inside" image. Verse 14 of the psalm says it this way: "My strength is gone, gone like water spilled on the ground. All my bones are out of joint; my heart is like melted wax. My throat is as dry as dust, and my tongue sticks to the roof of my mouth. You have left me for dead in the dust." I'll come back to this Psalm and others when I deal with spirituality and depression.

Generally people fighting depression are amazed and somewhat comforted to find how accurately such an old text describes what it feels like for them to wrestle with the illness. When they're depressed and hurting, it's always comforting to find that someone, even the ancient psalmist, knows how it feels in the thick of such a fight. Then, if I or someone else can recommend the psalm, at least maybe I have some clue about what they're feeling. The depressed person begins to get the message that they're not quite so alone in their illness. Maybe there is some way to make sense of the mystery that enshrouds them. Maybe there is hope.

The "inside" of depression is hard for teens and adults to describe and understand. Sometimes there is some crisis or event that happens and the person begins to feel very differently afterwards. Usually that kind of onset makes it easier to understand the changes brought about by the illness. The presence of a triggering event helps it make more sense as to why the depressed person feels so differently after the event. It's easier to understand what's going on with the depressed person if the feelings after the event can be contrasted with feelings before the triggering event. For most, however, the changes brought about by depression come on gradually and are much trickier to describe. They cannot point to any event and identify it as the trigger for their plunge into the valley of darkness.

When asked about the onset of their depression, a lot of teens can only give vague answers. The depressed teens say they started to notice that things just didn't come as easily for them as they did at some earlier point in their lives. Everything became more of a struggle. Making friends seemed to take more effort. Following directions at home seemed more difficult. They felt sluggish and were often accused of being lazy. It was harder not to get an "attitude." It became more difficult to be in a good mood. School became more and more "boring" (the word almost every depressed teen I've talked with has used).

When depressed teens use the word "boring" to describe school it confuses adults. As adults, we know that lots of things we have to do in our day-to-day lives are boring, but we still have to do them. We wonder why the depressed teen doesn't grasp this concept. Why don't they just buckle down and get it done, boring or not? Better yet, if they're bored, let's give them more things to do so they won't feel so bored.

Don't get me wrong. I remember some pretty boring classes in school. Some of the boredom was the fault of the subject matter and my particular interest (or lack thereof), and some of it was the fault of a few teachers. Let's face it, some people can take the most exciting things and make them truly boring. (I know a few preachers who would also fit that description, but that's another book.)

I think the depressed teens have taught me that when they use the word "boring," they mean something a little different. They're trying to describe a few difficult aspects of the depression. First, it becomes harder to stay focused, even when that's exactly what you're trying to do. The mind wanders more easily. Sometimes the depressed teens just completely "zone out." They don't really hear what's going on. Then they "wake up" at the end of the class only to realize they don't know how to do what was just explained. That means they won't be able to do the homework as easily, which probably means it will be even more overwhelming . . . which probably means the homework won't be done at all. Then they'll be further in the grade hole and have to struggle harder to make it up. Then they'll feel overwhelmed by the struggle to dig themselves out of the grade pit, so they'll shut down, do nothing and get deeper in the hole . . . and so on . . . and so on . . . and so on.

Another part of the "boring" feeling is the sense of lethargy and numbness that many experience who are fighting depression. It makes them feel like they're slogging through quicksand. They feel emotionally worn out and physically tired or exhausted. Everything seems to take more and more of the sparse supply of energy they possess. They can feel numb.

Remember what it was like the last time you had a really bad cold or flu? Your nose was stopped up, your throat was scratchy, and your taste buds were taking a vacation on some sunny warm beach without you. When you finally felt well enough to eat something, you couldn't taste anything. Talk about frustrating! You could eat your most favorite food in the entire world and still not taste it. You knew you were eating your favorite food and should taste something, but nothing was getting through from your tongue to your brain. That's one way to describe this numbness associated with depression. You go through the motions of living, but nothing gets through.

Remember the last visit to the dentist when she numbed your mouth? If it worked the way it was supposed to, you were safe. Hopefully the dentist could drill, cut, tug or pull and none of the pain would register in your brain. You could feel pressure against your skin, but not much else. Thank God! When you're numb physically, none of the normal physical sensations get through to your brain.

When you're numb from depression, nothing gets through. That's true for emotions, and sometimes even physical sensations. That's why it's easier to engage in acts of self-mutilation. The depression numbs the pain. Even when they're doing something that's supposed to feel "fun," the depressed person can't feel it. They go through the motions, but fail to feel even the good feelings.

People joining the depressed teen in fun activities may start to notice that the teen is not having as much fun. This generally prompts questions like, "What's wrong? Why aren't you having a good time? Why aren't you enjoying being with me? Why don't you appreciate what I'm doing for you?" This might cause more discomfort, so the depressed teen starts to avoid contacts. That way they don't have to face the questions. Then they feel more isolated, an even more depressing predicament, and so on . . . and so on . . . and so on. Down and down and down they go.

Irritability and reactive anger, even rage, are part of the struggle for many depressed youth. It feels like more little things bother them, and bigger things bother them even more. In other words, little things that another might shrug off and say, "What's the big deal?" register as irritation on the screen of the depressed teen. In some ways the depressed teen feels very little. They're numb. In other ways they feel too much.

Remember the last outing to the beach when you spent too much time having fun in the sun and baked yourself to a crisp? You went inside, showered, and changed. Then, that first moment you stepped back into the sun you experienced a real awakening. Gentle sunlight fell upon your skin. Normally you might welcome it as a comfortable experience. Now, with freshly charbroiled skin, you greet the same gentle sunlight with shrieks of pain. Suddenly the gentle rays feel like a blowtorch glowing red hot against your skin. You feel the same sunlight as before the sunburn, but with the sunburn you feel it so much that it's intensely painful. Feeling that kind of pain, you scream, yell, run for the car, or do whatever else is possible to avoid the painful sunrays.

This sunburn analogy is one way of grasping the idea that teens fighting depression feel some things too much. That's why they seem to "overreact" to the same stimuli experienced by others. They are not really "over reacting." They are actually trying to deal with an intensity of feeling that others are not experiencing. The teens are suffering from "emotional sunburns." They feel too much and respond out of their pain in ways that are sometimes inappropriate and hurtful. Before going on, let's stretch the sunburn analogy just a little further.

Suppose you're in that parking lot with the sunburn, you make the mad dash for your car to avoid the pain, and accidentally step on the toe of a stranger standing nearby as you race for relief. The stranger might not take the time to put all the pieces together and figure, "Ah, they must have a whopper of a sunburn and are trying to get out of the sun. I'll try to be understanding and not get upset with them." No, there's a better chance that in that squished-toe moment the stranger will wince with pain, and shout something through clenched teeth like, "You jerk!" or worse.

"I'm sorry," you might cry over your shoulder as you close the car door. Your glance at the stranger shows the offered apology fell on a deaf ear and you wonder to yourself, "Why don't they realize I was hurting and only trying to get away from the pain? Why don't they realize my stepping on their toe was an accident? I would never "try" to hurt them. I'm not that kind of person!"

You see the point, don't you? When teens begin to feel the effects of the depression and sometimes react in strange ways to deal with the pain, their actions can often be more reflexive than planned, and consequently misinterpreted. They react to the pain by either trying to avoid it completely, or getting away from it once it's struck. In the process they might accidentally hurt others around them. The others might easily think the teen "meant" to hurt them. If we're not careful and observant, we might be too quick to cry, "You jerk!" as the teen runs to their sanctuary and slams the door behind them.

This heightened intensity from the illness can amplify other feelings in addition to irritability and anger. It can also amplify sadness, loneliness, and anxiety, just to name a few. This extra intensity leads to that feeling of being overwhelmed that I've mentioned before. Depressed and anxious teens are easily overwhelmed. Things that would not trigger a similar response in others set off a powerful feeling of being overwhelmed in depressed teens. That feeling of being overwhelmed is not a very comfortable experience. Do you remember the last time you felt it? Didn't it make you want to get rid of it somehow? Didn't you want to run for the car when you had the sunburn?

When a depressed teen feels overwhelmed, they don't normally say to themselves, "Hmm, I think I'm feeling overwhelmed." In fact, one of the goals of therapy with depressed teens is to help them consciously identify the feeling of being overwhelmed and take healthy steps to respond. However, before they've been educated about their illness, the depressed teens just know they feel something very uncomfortable and want to escape its hold. They do whatever they can to rid themselves of the feeling.

We call that act of trying to avoid or rid themselves of the painful feeling a "defense." Their favorite defense might be that flash of anger, or withdrawal, some sort of shutdown, or some other form of escape like alcohol or other drugs. It's not a rational, thought-out process. The depressed teens just do it, because somehow it makes them feel better in the moment (just like you dashed for the car and stepped on the stranger's toe). A shutdown is another form of defense. The shutdown is often the depressed teen's preferred response to feeling overwhelmed by school and homework.

Here's how the shutdown defense might go. The teen "zones out" or has difficulty concentrating in class. They miss a lot of the explanations for the homework. They go home and open the book. Then they start to realize they may not know how to do the work, or they may understand it, but it feel like there is so much homework that they will never be able to finish. The response then is usually, "I'll never be able to finish all of this. It will take forever; so why bother?" They close the book, lie about doing the work when quizzed by a parent, and go off to school to repeat the process the next day.

Eventually the depressed teen doesn't even bother to look at the book. They just "know" it will be overwhelming, so why bother? By the time a report card makes it home, the student is already in a deep, deep hole that further intensifies that sense of being overwhelmed. They continue to practice their defense on a daily basis because it momentarily keeps them from feeling that awful sense of being overwhelmed.

I don't think I'm a klutz, but my wife and kids have kidded me at times by saying they should call the hospital emergency room and reserve a bed before I start my next home repair or remodeling project. The truth is, I'm always so busy that I get in too much of a hurry. The results have been things like cutting off the tip of a finger, missing the board with the sledge hammer and hitting my leg, mashing fingers with hammers, having things come down on my foot. You get the picture. Do you remember the last time you smashed a finger? It's truly a weird sort of feeling. It hurts like crazy and has almost a numb feeling all at the same time.

That's the closest I can come to describing what I think depressed teens mean when they talk about that internal feeling of hurt, frustration, hopelessness, loneliness, despair, and numbness. This hurt and numbness can become so intense that the feelings can cause the teen to seek relief with defenses that generally take an even more destructive path. These more destructive defenses might include cutting themselves or other forms of self-mutilation, drug and alcohol use, eating disorders, promiscuous sex, shoplifting, and others.

I know all of these defenses sound irrational and destructive. They are irrational and very destructive, but the defensive acts still fulfill a purpose by momentarily managing the pain from the illness. Unless the depressed teen gets the right help, they often will continue to practice these more destructive defenses, gradually making them "bad habits" that can take on a life of their own and further complicate the depression.

There's yet another part of depression that's very important to understand. Depression changes how a person thinks. It doesn't mean that it makes them "crazy." On occasion, depression can become so severe that a person might have delusional thinking, but not in most cases. Here's the best way to describe what I mean about the change in thinking. Do you remember the old question, "Is the glass on the table half empty or half full?" According to the old theory, if you see the glass as half full, it means you tend to be a more optimistic person. Conversely, if you see the glass as half empty, it means you tend to be more pessimistic.

A teen who is depressed will always see the glass as half empty, and wonder why anyone could possibly think that it could ever be half full. In other words, everything tends to be shaded by severe pessimism. "I really am a terrible, worthless person. No one wants to be with me. No one understands me. There's no way I can do that. I'll never get what I want." These are just a few examples of how the thinking process is distorted by depression. In order to reach these teens, you have to be willing to recognize that this distorted, pessimistic view really does represent how they perceive the world. You can't simply tell them they're wrong and expect them to believe it. They don't see what you see. You see positive possibilities. The depressed teen sees only negative impossibilities.

Depression also changes thinking in a way that alters the teen's experience of time. This change in thinking about time contributes to the flood of despair in the depressed person. Aaron Beck, known by many as the father of cognitive therapy, called this experience the cognitive triad of depression.[1] He divides time into the past, present, and future. A person who is depressed knows they feel awful in the present. The depression makes it very difficult to remember past times that were good, so they have trouble remembering a day when they haven't felt the same awful depression. If the past and present have been one long awful feeling, then obviously (according to their depressed logic), tomorrow will be the same.

---

1. Beck, "Core Problem in Depression," 47–55.

The depression has a way of making them think that the past, present, and future have all melded into one. In other words, they feel awful now, they can't ever remember when it hasn't felt this bad, and that certainly means it will always feel this bad. The past, present, and future seem like one endless experience of despair, so why bother.

Depression can be horrific. However we try to describe it, the picture that emerges reveals a troubled sky filled with the storm clouds of chaotic feelings and thoughts. This constellation of feelings and thoughts can become the driving force for self-destructive behaviors. Sometimes the behaviors center around what we might call "thrill-seeking" activities. These thrill-seeking behaviors might include anything from bungee jumping to reckless driving. These various activities seem to have one thing in common. They give the teen that "high" which momentarily pushes the chaotic, troubling feelings aside.

The use of alcohol and drugs might be considered as thrill-seeking behavior. The drinking and drug use are often combined with other kinds of thrill-seeking activities at parties, etc. However, the alcohol and drugs serve another purpose in addition to providing a thrill. The alcohol and drugs also have a temporary anesthetic quality. They can provide a momentary relief from depression and anxiety for many teens who use the substances. The three most popular "anesthetic" drugs I've encountered with depressed teens are marijuana, nicotine, and alcohol.

This kind of drug use is very dangerous for depressed teens. They tend to start by telling themselves that they are just smoking some pot or drinking some alcohol to experiment like everyone else. (Note to teens: The notion that every teen experiments with alcohol and drugs is a myth that needs to be busted! *There are many teens who do not experiment with drugs and alcohol!*) What the depressed teen using drugs fails to notice is that they have moved beyond experimenting to plain old drug use. They hide the fact from themselves that they have begun to self-medicate with the drugs. Tom avoided the alcohol and marijuana, but succumbed to the cigarette smoking at his first job. He later gave up the habit as he began to recover from the depression.

The thirst to feel better can drive teens to even more desperate measures. Various forms of self-mutilation are sometimes practiced. These acts can include cutting, burning, piercing, or tattooing. Let me quickly say that I'm not bashing "professional" jewelry piercing or tattooing. I'm not talking about something you go to a store or establishment and have someone do to you. I'm talking about acts of self-mutilation that teens generally privately perform on themselves. They might cut their arms or other concealed parts of their bodies. They might burn themselves with cigarettes, etc. They might "scrape" insignia into their skin, creating their own tattoos.

These are not really suicidal gestures. That's what the teens have taught me. That's not to say the practices are not dangerous. The self-mutilating acts are extremely dangerous! There have been numerous occasions when people have been cutting to relieve pain and cut too deeply, creating life threatening situations. The hurting individuals probably didn't start the cutting with the conscious intent of killing themselves. They simply wanted relief from some of the pain.

Teens who self-mutilate are in serious trouble and need professional help. The teens tell me they cut or mutilate themselves because somehow it helps move some of the feelings or focus some of the pain. It's really difficult to explain its purpose, but those who practice some form of self-mutilation say it does do something that results in a moment of relief. Some say it stops the numbness they feel and helps demonstrate in a very tangible and visible way on the outside the severity of the pain they're experiencing on the inside. It's another one of those strange aspects of depression that is hard for us to understand, but it is some form of relief. Needless to say, like drugs, it's the wrong kind of relief. It's merely a temporary "fix" that leads to more difficulties as the journey through the illness continues.

If depression or its relatives continue long enough, they can lead to even more serious situations. They can lead to death. Suicide is a very, very real threat when teens become depressed. In my experience, I've found that people wind up killing themselves along a couple of different patterns.

One suicidal situation arises when the depression has worn the depressed person down to the point that they are just totally exhausted. They fit the description of the psalmist when he said he felt left for dead. These souls live in daily agony. At some earlier point in their journey they probably would have said that they would never kill themselves. They know it would hurt people they love too much, and that thought serves as enough of a deterrent to prevent them from acting on their suicidal thoughts. However, after they hurt for so long, nothing else matters except finding a way to make the pain go away.

The depressed person begins to believe that there is only one escape from their despair and pain—death. Even the fact that they know their death might hurt others is no longer enough to stop them. Sometimes they are even able to rationalize that the initial pain others will experience from their death will be outweighed by the relief their friends and family will gain from no longer having the "burden" of the depressed person weighing upon them. Of course, this dangerous rationalization is simply part of the distorted thinking from the depression.

The depressed, suicidal people I've been describing are the ones who "plan" their escape. They may even become temporarily relieved and "lighter" in the time leading up to their suicide, because the awareness of their eventual escape gives them a sense of freedom. I remember one day when a very depressed mother came into my counseling office for her weekly visit just a few days before Thanksgiving. This week she seemed happier than I had ever seen her.

As we talked I began to have a strange sense that this young mother had made a plan to kill herself, and that I was witnessing her momentary relief before she performed the deadly act. I told her of my suspicion and asked her if it was accurate. She quickly and matter-of-factly admitted that my suspicion was correct. She had indeed made a plan to send her children to her mother's for the holiday and kill herself while the children were away. She thought I should be able to see the logic of it and agree with her that it was the best plan for her life. At first she wasn't too thrilled that I disagreed with her logic. We spent the rest of the session arranging alternatives. She lived.

If a teen is depressed, warning signs that he or she is playing with the idea of suicide might begin to emerge before the teen reaches the stage of actively planning to kill themselves. These early warning signs might include their researching and reading about death, writing or creating artwork about death, talking about death or threatening to hurt themselves, or even suicidal gestures like overdoses of aspirin or other medications. If teens show some of the other signs of depression already mentioned and begin to talk about death or show their writings and artwork about death to parents, teachers, or friends, care should be taken to get the teen some professional help.

Depressed teens can move beyond the lower level threat of thinking about suicide to a much higher level of threat as they begin to actively plan their suicide. Their feelings of helplessness and hopelessness push them from dropping hints in their writings and conversations to behaviors much like the ones I described in the woman above, who came to my office before Thanksgiving. The behaviors of the teens can include exhibiting that same sudden sense of relief I described in the young mother, giving things away to others, saying special goodbyes to people, or putting all their things in order.

If the depressed teen can tell you how they might kill themselves, it probably means they've given suicide some conscious thought, and are at a higher risk of carrying it out. If they know of other friends or family members who have committed suicide, this also places the depressed teen at higher risk of trying it themselves. These teens should not be left alone. They need immediate help. Don't be afraid to take them to the nearest hospital emergency room if necessary. Don't let the depressed teen talk you out of your concern.

I think there is also a different kind of suicide. I would say it's a more impulsive type with very little forewarning. The person might have felt depressed and bad for a while, but had never gone so far as to make a plan. Then one day they might be driving down the road and have a thought like, "I feel awful. Maybe I should just drive this car into a telephone pole." Maybe they do, or maybe they don't. Sometimes they may simply get a rush of overwhelming emotions that push them to perform a suicidal gesture like taking an overdose of pills. The act is far more impulsive and reflexive than planned.

Sometimes the actual thought of killing themselves might even be less conscious. They might feel really bad, but have no conscious plan for suicide. However, they might just "accidentally" walk too close to the highway one night and wind up being hit by a car. They might just "accidentally" have a fatal car crash because they were driving too fast. Was it really accidental? Keep an eye out when teens engage in risky and dangerous activities, especially if they're doing risky things without proper safety equipment. They might be giving you clues that they're feeling pretty depressed and don't care much about the potentially fatal consequences of their activities.

When we hear of a teen that has committed suicide, our hearts ache. Sometimes we acknowledge to ourselves that it really doesn't surprise us to hear of the death. Maybe the teen seemed really emotionally troubled, or was in and out of trouble at school or in the community. More often, I think it does surprise us to hear that a teen has committed suicide. If we look back, we might see a few warning signs. The truth is, we missed it.

They seemed like they had so much going for them. How could they want to die? How could they take their own life?

My first experience with the suicide of a peer came when I was in college. I was home for the summer. My mother woke me one morning with this news: a friend and gifted musician I had performed with for years had killed himself. He was one of the most incredible musicians I had ever met. At the funeral one of his relatives told me that my friend's band had been on the road and was just about to hit the big time in Las Vegas. Everything was looking great for him. Why now? Why ever? Sometimes it can be really difficult to see it coming.

Depression and its cronies can be killers in one way or another. Besides the suicides, we have the accidental deaths that are directly related to the mental health conditions. There are the car accidents involving alcohol, drugs, or just reckless driving. There are the drug and alcohol overdoses. There are the murders and other violent crimes related to these illnesses. We must take these illnesses seriously. I've buried more than one teen whose death was related to depression. I almost buried my own son.

We were well into the downslide of Tom's depression. More and more school was being missed. He had less and less contact with his friends. We struggled to keep him moving at all. He spent lots of time in his room alone, lying on the bed with the covers pulled up and his face to the wall. One night my wife and I had just turned off our bedroom light and were starting to fall asleep. I heard the downstairs door to the outside close.

The sound of the door really didn't alarm me. Tom's room was on the ground level below us. Every evening he let the dogs back inside before he went to bed. I simply assumed I was hearing the sound of the usual routine. That couldn't have been further from the truth!

The next morning I went downstairs and found Tom lying on the sofa in the family room. That was unusual. Sometimes during the day he hung out in that room, but almost every night he retreated to his own room and bed. Then I noticed a piece of paper lying on a table at the end of the sofa near his feet. I picked up the paper and saw that it was a note that began in big letters, "Read Me." By the time I finished the note from Tom, I was shaking so hard I could barely stand. Here's what he wrote that took my breath away:

"In case you didn't know at 1:00 last night I ran away to escape my feelings. I would have been gone for good, except I fell in a creek and when the water formed ice I got a little cold and came in at 4:00. Since that didn't work I would like you to tell everybody I know to tell everyone else I am dead to the world. No one will call or come see me, cause no one cares. I am now isolating myself from everyone. Sometimes I'll write a note like this, but most of the time I won't communicate at all. Go ahead and give this note to B (his closest friend)."

If I had any doubts about the validity of his story, they were quickly swept away when I looked in his bathroom and saw a wet pile of clothes on the floor. We almost lost him for good. He was still alive, but, in his words, "dead to the world." Remember Psalm 22? "You have left me for dead in the dust." I told you these illnesses could be killers. Patti and I thought we knew what to look for. We were trying everything we knew to help, but we still missed it. It happened so quickly that we didn't see his act of desperation coming. However, our response to it is worth noting.

When we realized what had happened that night, Patti and I didn't respond with anger and punishment. We didn't ground Tom for leaving the house in the middle of the night. This wasn't an act of rebellion or teenage mischief. This was an act of desperation and a warning sign that Tom was in a particularly low period of depression. We acknowledged it was a warning sign and took the appropriate steps to help him manage his depression.

Depression brings with it a lot of internal conflict. Depressed teens want to do well, but they can't. They want to belong, but it seems like it takes so much energy, so they don't. They want to know what's getting in their way, but they can't figure it out. They want others to understand, but they can't seem to make it happen. They want to succeed, but fail at every turn. They want to be "good" but do the wrong things that cause hurt and trouble for themselves and others. They want to get along with their parents and family, but say and do the very things that result in more alienation.

Parents who bring their depressed teens to my office often complain that the teen has become for the rest of the family almost intolerable to live with. These are often the teens I mentioned before who have that, "I'm just waiting for you to join the rest and tell me I'm a screw-up" look in their eyes. The stories are always different, but bear a striking similarity. The stories don't make sense. What I mean is that it just doesn't make sense that a teen would want to be that bad, when they know the rewards they might garner by being good. That's the tip off. That's what tells me that the teen is not "acting out." He or she is reacting to something. The teen is being driven by something.

When Tom was depressed, he would become angry and irrational and then do something wrong that he knew would only further complicate his life. Patti and I began to understand that when these irrational events happened, he was in that "altered state of consciousness." He was being flooded with too much emotional stimulus, and was truly out of control. By the grace of God, we figured out that he wasn't trying to hurt us. Rather, Tom was being driven by something to hurt us.

After I've listened to the story of the parents and a depressed teen sitting in my counseling office whose illness is driving the teen to irrational statements and actions, I'll turn to the teen and say, "You really don't want to act this way do you?" At first I might get a smirk from the teen or a smart retort like, "What do you think?" Then I continue. "Look, I get it. I know your secret. You don't really want to hurt your parents. You go from being okay to feeling enraged in a split second. The awful words are out of your mouth before you have a chance to think about them. It's like something is driving you. Then, after the hurtful words have come out, you feel bad that you've said them. You actually feel bad that you've hurt them, but you can't admit it or get them to believe it. Right?"

If I had video cameras to tape the faces of the teen and their parents as I'm saying that to the teen, here's what you'd see in many cases. The teen's hardened challenging smirk slowly starts to fade. Their eyes begin to widen like teacups. In those surprised eyes you can see the question starting to form. "How did you know that secret? How did you know that about me." Then, the teacups begin to spill over as the tears run down their face. I mean it. I've had some of the toughest acting teenage boys begin to weep as they start to realize that someone finally has a clue about what has been going on inside them.

As the parents are listening and observing, their faces also begin to change. The frustration and anger focused in their brows fade to a question mark and doubt. "What is this guy talking about?" I can hear their eyes shouting, "Is he crazy? I live with this kid. I know how awful they've been." But as the tears begin to trickle down the face of their teen, the parents see the genuineness of the response. The parents are still puzzled, but generally soften a bit as they realize something important has just happened in the step toward healing.

Maybe the moment in my office helps the parents start to trust their son or daughter just a little more. Trust is so important in this fight. Parents, you really must try to trust that your teen is doing his or her best to understand what's happening to them. You must trust that your teen is fighting the monster the best they are able. Teens, it is critical that you do your best in the struggle with the depression. You cannot use your fight with the monster as a way to manipulate your parents. If your parents know you're doing your best, it's easier for them to help you through the nightmare.

Trust is a very precious gift. Unfortunately, people often come to that realization after they've done something to lose trust. Be careful. Try not to lose trust in one another. However, if trust is broken in some way, it can be rebuilt. Don't ever think it's too late to rebuild trust in a relationship. It may take time and lots of hard work, but it is possible in many situations!

Music has always been important in our family. My daughter, Rebekah, and I play musical instruments, Patti sings in choirs, and Tom has an incredible love and appreciation for music. He has amassed quite a collection of CDs, and has deejayed on a few occasions. Music has been one way that we've connected. From time to time Tom or Rebekah will bring me a CD and say, "Hey dad, you've got to hear this." I love it! Metallica has been one of Tom's favorite groups. Not long ago they released a new CD called "St. Anger." Tom bought a copy and said, "Dad you've got to listen to this. It's one of the best descriptions of teenage depression I've found." He didn't have to say that twice to get my attention!

By the way, one of the reasons that teens listen to music that parents feel might be depressing is because the teens hear some of their own story in the lyrics. I don't believe the songs depress the teens. I think the songs are cathartic for the teens. The intensity of the music helps move the feelings trapped inside the depressed youth. The teens also identify with many of the ideas and feelings expressed in the lyrics of the songs. The lyrics are like a modern day version of Psalm 22. (If the psalmist lived today, would he be a heavy-metal rocker, a rapper, or some other "poet" of the teen culture?)

The lyrics of the songs help the depressed teens believe they're not alone. Maybe someone else does understand. The loud, raucous nature of the music can also be helpful for breaking through some of the numbness in a way that's not self-destructive (as long as they're not destroying their eardrums with the volume). There are a lot of things like their music that I may not always enjoy, understand, or agree with. However, I've tried to listen as teens have taught me how the various things are helpful. That's part of what I'm passing along in these pages.

Anyway, when Tom said that to me about the new Metallica CD, you can bet my ears perked up. The song he was bringing to my attention is a pretty loud and raucous song called "Invisible Kid." One line of the lyrics says, "I'm OK, just go away, I'm OK, please don't stray too far."[2] Roughly paraphrased, the lyrics say something like, "Get away from me and leave me alone, but don't go too far." The meaning behind the lyrics illustrates the internal conflict I was talking about.

Depressed teens are often telling adults to leave them alone. Too often, the parents of the depressed teen see the angry teen telling them to get out of their face, but don't hear the unspoken part, "but don't go too far." It can be really, really hard to hear the "but don't go too far" part. Lots of things can get in the way of it being heard, either from the side of the parent, or the teen. But trust me, the hope that the parent will not go too far is really there!

Teens really need their parents. Don't let them fool you. Teens want to be independent. As a matter of fact, we raise them to learn to become independent. It's often a frustrating struggle for the teen and the parents. Many times I've looked at a teen in my office and said, "It's really frustrating, isn't it? Adults tell you to grow up and learn to make your own decisions. Then when you decide to make one, we tell you it's the wrong one." The teen usually smiles and vigorously nods his or her head in agreement.

It's tough but very important for teens to work out how they will learn to make more of their own decisions with the "input" from their parents. In a way, it's like learning how to "need" your parents in yet another new way. I remember on several occasions when one of my children learned to do something for him- or herself and didn't need me to do it for them anymore. Whether it was turning a water faucet on or driving them to their friend's house, each new learned task meant they didn't need me in quite the same way. However, it didn't mean they no longer needed me in their lives for anything.

The teen years bring a lot of the changes that make it necessary for teens and parents to renegotiate how parents are "needed." All these changes can sometimes cause parents to feel like they're being pushed away

2. Metallica, "Invisible Kid."

so much that they miss that unspoken lyric from before ("but don't go too far"). Teens still need their parents. Depressed teens need their parents even more, even though they may be the teens that look outwardly like they're trying the hardest to push their parents away.

The moments I've just described in my office when depressed teens first start to reveal the secrets of their struggle are often the first time parents hear that hidden phrase in the lyrics of the song their child has been screaming in their faces ("don't go too far"). Back up, parents, but don't go too far. Be ready. Your teen needs you! You can help carry the light they need in the darkness.

3

Wrestling Holds
to Use (on Parents)

Equipping Ourselves for the Journey

ONE DAY I was serving on a panel discussion about counseling teens and their parents. The group asked me to speak regarding my work with parents. I began by saying, "Basically, you can use a full nelson or a half nelson [wrestling holds] on the parent. I prefer the half nelson because that frees up one hand to give "noogies" to the top of the parent's scalp at the same time." At first they probably thought I was crazy. The remark was greeted with inquisitive looks until I explained that often when working with teens and their parents, the first thing I have to do is pull the parents off the teen.

As Tom's depression worsened, he missed more and more school. My wife was working as a night-shift nurse, and I worked days and evenings as a pastoral counselor. That meant it was my job to get our son and daughter up and off to school each morning. I began to dread the trek from my morning cup of coffee in the kitchen to Tom's room downstairs. I was afraid of what I would find. What scared me most was finding the same scenario I had found morning after morning after morning.

The ritual would go something like this: I would walk into Tom's room and find him still on his bed, even if his alarm had gone off. My line was, "Tom, it's time to get up for school." His response was, more often than not, the same, "I can't go. I'm sick." That's the short version. I'll spare you all the variations like, "Why can't you go?" "I don't know." "What's wrong, why are you sick, what hurts?" "I don't know," and on, and on, and on, and on.

At the end of each morning's script, my response would be the same. I would become very angry. I've confessed to many that I became so angry I wanted to pick up Tom and throw him through the wall. I'm not kid ding. I was that angry. At first the anger pushed me to verbally prod him even more. I would stand there in his room and nag, then threaten, then yell. Once I even tried physically pulling him from his bed just to get him on his feet.

It seems stupid and irrational, doesn't it, to stand there and yell like that. I mean, first I was yelling at someone I loved, someone I would defend with my own life if anyone tried to hurt him. Second, I was standing there yelling at someone who had just told me they felt sick. No matter how you look at my response and try to rationalize it, the conclusion is the same. I was acting stupid and irrational. There I was, this highly educated, compassionate person, known by others for his patience, yelling at my son who had just told me he felt ill.

Tom was very persistent. None of my "verbal interventions" worked. As a matter of fact, as the ritual was repeated, it took a shorter and shorter amount of time for me to hit the anger point. The morning confrontation always ended the same. I would speak my lines then turn and leave the room. I was so angry that I was afraid if I stayed, I might try to pull Tom from the bed and one or both of us would get hurt in the almost inevitable fight. I was also afraid I might just pick him up and throw him against the wall in his bedroom.

I have to digress here for just a moment and tell you how the kind of pain Tom went through can cause a sort of amnesia. One day a few years ago, after Tom had recovered from the depression, I asked him what his mother and I might have done differently that would have been more helpful during his struggle. This was a point in time when Tom was not yet ready to talk much about what had happened to him. He paused for a moment then almost annoyingly said, "Maybe you could have pushed more." I bit my tongue to stifle a laugh or a rebuttal. All I could think of were those mornings in his room when I stood there like an irrational madman, verbally pushing so hard, and feeling so angry, that I wanted to throw him through the wall.

One day yet another depressed teen and her parents walked into my office for the first time. The parents began the unfortunately all-too-familiar script about how she would not follow their directions. Every time she disobeyed, they took away something of hers and put it in a garbage bag. This routine had been repeated until every single thing the teen owned except for a couple of pairs of blue jeans and a couple of shirts, was in a garbage bag. Her room had been completely stripped. Even the posters and other decorations in her room had been removed from the walls and placed in the garbage bags.

I try to respect parents' feelings and authority so later in the interview I asked the teen to leave the room. I didn't want to embarrass the parents in front of their daughter when I asked about the garbage bags. As soon as the teen walked out the parents continued to voice their frustration with her. Finally, I asked them about the garbage bags. I told them that in and of itself, taking something away as a consequence is not necessarily a bad thing. However, in this case, I had one question. "Did it work?" They looked sheepishly at me and admitted that it had made no difference.

Teens have actually told me that when parents get into this kind of struggle, the teen will say to him- or herself, "Go ahead! Take it away. I can handle it." I call this a "bunker mentality." The teen emotionally hunkers down deeper into the safety of their foxhole or bunker, waiting for the parents to try their next "shot." The teen finds some pleasure in watching their parents dangle from the string of irrationality over the well of insanity. The whole thing usually continues in some sort of dance that results in an uncomfortable, unhelpful, and even dangerous stalemate between the teen and the parents.

Einstein's definition of *insanity* is repeating the same thing over and over, each time expecting a different result.[1] I've talked with a lot of "insane" parents, and for a while, I was one of them. There I was, standing in the middle of Tom's room, daily dipping deeply into the well of "insanity." I kept repeating the ritual over and over and over, each day hoping something would change. It never did. One day the anger came so quickly in the ritual, that I reached that point where I knew I needed to leave almost immediately after walking into Tom's room. I turned and walked back upstairs after barely uttering my fist line. I could see the response on Tom's face before I heard it come from his mouth.

From that day forward, the ritual changed. I walked downstairs, announced my opening line, and then retreated back upstairs. I hadn't figured out anything at that point; I just knew I was too angry to stand there and try to talk at that moment. I've jokingly told folks there was a path worn from Tom's room to the upstairs, where I would retreat to in order to avoid more hurt. I was kidding about the worn path, but not about the intensity of my anger.

1. Einstein, "Brainy Quote," line 1.

There are two really vital points that need to be made here. God gave me the strength and insight to do two important things. First, I knew not to step over a certain line when I got angry, even as I daily repeated the same ritual. We are all capable of hurting each other very badly if we reach a certain level of anger. I've seen really good people in my office who have reported how they hurt each other time and again. They surprised themselves that they were capable of such hurt. They allowed themselves to step over the line.

Good people are not immune from hurting others. Sometimes we fail to pay attention to warning signs that our anger is bubbling and has the potential to take us to a place where we might hurt someone, even someone we love. Anger is very seductive. It keeps pulling us into its embrace, promising a relief from our frustration and pain if we will only drink its intoxicating brew and spew it on the other.

I think another reason anger gets the best of many people is that they rely too much on willpower. This applies not only to anger but also other habits or behaviors that someone is trying to avoid. Here's what I mean. Think of willpower as a fire extinguisher on the wall. Fire extinguishers are great. You want them where you might need them in case of a fire. You hope they're charged and ready to go if the need ever arises. However, the real point is that you never want to use them. In other words, you want to practice good habits so you don't start fires in the first place. That way you'll never be put in the position of wondering if the fire extinguisher you pick up in the moment of crisis is charged and capable of extinguishing the flames you've created.

Willpower works the same. The point is you really never want to have to use it. Instead, you should try to live your life in such a way as to avoid crisis situations where the only thing left to rely on is your willpower. Maybe your willpower will save you in the moment, or maybe it will fail you. You'll never know until it's too late.

Let me give an example I often use. I love ice cream. I don't *like* it. I *love* it. As a matter of fact, I love it too much. I've been around long enough to know that if I go to the store and buy a half-gallon container of ice cream, the contents will not go to waste in my freezer at home. I won't eat it all at once, but I will finish the half-gallon of ice cream in a few days. That's too much ice cream for me. I know (from experience) that my willpower will not protect me from that ice cream lurking in my freezer. I can hear it calling me. Instead of fighting the urge to visit the freezer, I've learned not to buy the ice cream and take it home in the first place. That's the point where I know I can win the battle. After that, if the ice cream is in the freezer, my chances of getting my willpower to keep me from eating it are pretty slim to none.

Don't let the fact that my example is about ice cream detract from the importance of this principle. Don't rely on your willpower to save you from hurting someone with your anger. Learn your limits and withdraw before the fire starts and you have only the fire extinguisher to rely upon. I believe that almost everyone, if pushed to a certain limit, is capable of hurting someone else very badly. I learned this about my own self very early in my ministry, when I was serving my first charge (three churches) as a pastor.

I've never really been a physically violent person. I had my last physical scuffle with another boy when I was about seven. I came from a part of the country where there was a lot of violence. My hometown is where the Hatfield and McCoy families conducted their feud. My paternal grandfather was a coal miner and helped organize the union. That was a very violent struggle. When I was young, I saw him get into a physical brawl with two of my older cousins. He held his own against them. He was a big man who could be violent. I was told that he was known for being able to pick a man up over his shoulders and heave him aside.

Later in my life my father admitted that his father had been verbally and physically abusive to his family. My father spent his life working (successfully) not to be like his father. Dad and Mom taught me to avoid physical violence if at all possible, so I never thought of myself as a "physical" kind of person. I figured it just wasn't in me. Then Patti and I had Tom, our firstborn.

One night shortly after we brought Tom home from the hospital, I was up with him in the middle of the night. I had just put him back in his bed when I heard a sound in the house. I knew it was just the strong wind outside rattling a loose window, but I had the strangest, startling sensation. What if it was someone in the house? What if they tried to get near my son? What if they tried to hurt him? I "felt" the answer to my questions jolt me like the ending of a roller coaster. I knew what I would do. I would rip the intruder to shreds with my bare hands! I knew what I was capable of. There was no denying it. If provoked, I could be just like my grandfather.

Maybe that was preparation for later in Tom's teen years when I stood in his room each morning feeling my anger start to consume me. All I know is that as I stood in my teen's room, God helped me remember what I was capable of, so I left. I hadn't figured anything out at that point. I had no clue about how to change Tom's mind about going to school. I didn't feel any less angry. I simply knew I had to leave Tom's room, because I knew what I was capable of if I let things go too far. I couldn't count on the "fire extinguisher" (my willpower) to save us. I knew I had to leave before the flames got started.

Some mornings I was better at leaving than other mornings. Most of the time I just left. A few times I still had to dip into the well of insanity, and try to threaten or yell just a little to convince myself of how powerless I really was at that moment. Eventually, I just left. I got better and better at leaving sooner rather than later.

I said there were two important things God taught me in that act of walking away from Tom's room. The first was to acknowledge my ability to reach a level of anger that could become destructive and to avoid reaching that point. The second was to acknowledge the insanity of my actions and stop the ritual even though I didn't know what else to do. It was only then that Patti and I began to have the insights that proved most helpful for Tom and us as we continued in the journey.

There is a modern version of the Hippocratic oath that many medical students take upon graduation. The oath, written by Louis Lasagna in 1964, says at one point, "I will not be ashamed to say 'I know not,' nor will I fail to call in my colleagues when the skills of another are needed for a patient's recovery."[2] If we paraphrased this for parents, it might read something like this. "If I find that I'm doing the same thing over and over and it's not working, I'll stop, even if I don't know what else to do. I'll say, 'I don't know,' and ask for help. I won't repeatedly do the same thing that's proven unhelpful and probably reached the point of hurting the relationship between me and my child . . . even if it feels like it will kill me to stop." Wait a minute. What is that "it-might-kill-me-to-stop" feeling? What's going on there?

The break from the insanity came when God gave me the courage to stop doing the same thing over and over, even though I didn't know what else to do. It did almost feel like it would kill me to stop the ritual. There was some powerful feeling that was driving me to repeat the unhelpful be-

2. Lasagna, "Modern Hippocratic Oath," 7.

haviors. There was something that was driving me to the anger. There was something I had to confront. God gave me the courage to admit I didn't know what to do, and stop the hurtful rituals. (There were other things we were trying in addition to the morning ritual that were just as unhelpful.) Only when I risked admitting I didn't know what to do and stopped the hurtful rituals, did I then begin to understand the workings of the most powerful demon I had to face—*fear!*

When I teach marriage seminars, I love to read aloud the following quote and ask the couples if they know the source. Usually I get answers like, "Churchill," or "Roosevelt," or even "Oprah." They are always surprised to hear the real source. The quote goes like this: "Fear is the path to the dark-side. Fear leads to anger, anger leads to hate, and hate leads to suffering."[3] Did you guess? The answer is, Yoda, the wise little green guy from the *Star Wars* epic tale. How true it is. How evident it must be if Hollywood writers know it, yet how difficult it is for most of us to find. It's almost as though we have to rediscover it for each of ourselves. The driving force behind the kind of anger I was experiencing was fear— no, probably more like terror. I was scared to death.

What was I afraid of? You name it! What was happening to Tom? What would happen if he wouldn't go to school? Would the school system send him into the truancy department? Would they send him to juvenile detention for not going to school? What would happen if he didn't graduate? Would his life be ruined forever? Was Tom going to survive this? Was he going to hurt himself? What would his friends think about him? What impact was this having on his younger sister? What would people think about Patti and me as parents? What would people think about me as a counselor if they knew my own son was going through something like this? Would people quit bringing their teens to me for help? Would people in general stop coming to me for help? What would I do if no one came to me for counseling? How could I make a living? How could I support my family? (This is the short list of the fear driven questions!)

It was fear! That's what was driving me to act insanely angry toward Tom! I wasn't really angry with Tom. He was scaring me to death. Better yet, the illness that tried to take him from us was scaring me to death! That awareness became the turning point in our struggle. It wasn't Tom that was scaring me. It was the illness that was terrifying me. It was *it!* This awareness enabled me one morning to walk into Tom's room and say to

3. Lucas, *Star Wars: Episode 1.*

him, "Look son, we're not fighting each other here. We're fighting *it!* I'm not pushing you. I'm pushing against *it!* Let's not fight against each other. Let's fight together against *it!*"

I could see the recognition in his face. Tom understood what I was trying to say. That mutual acknowledgement that we were fighting *it* instead of each other became a critical tool we used in all of our subsequent conversations. That conversation didn't fix everything, but it made a huge difference in how the relationship Tom had with Patti and me survived during the arduous journey. I'm convinced that good relationships Tom shared with Patti and me and important others in his life were probably the key component in his recovery.

Thus far, this entire chapter has been the setup for this one point. If parents are to be helpful to their teens going through an illness like depression, the parents must be willing to face their own demons and have a radical change of perspective. If parents want to be helpful, they must stop the insanity of the anger and frustration in order to face their fear. In facing that fear they must come to the realization that this is not their child they are fighting, it is a terrible medical illness that has the capacity to steal life. *It* has the ability to push the teen to do and say things the teen might not ordinarily do or say. They must learn to fight *it* together, instead of fighting each other.

The parents must get to the root of their fear in order that they might find hope. They must face the darkness in order to find the light. They must experience the "death" of their typical ways of viewing the struggles of their child if they and their child are to find "resurrection." They must face all of this if they are to have the courage to take the risks necessary to help their child. The root of the fear is something that confronts us more often than we would like to admit. The root of our fear is the awareness of our limits. We feel vulnerable as well as helpless, and it scares us to death.

I have often kidded people and said that hospitals really set us up when we see that newborn cherub in their bassinet. There's almost always a little blue or pink tag with the newborn child's name neatly inscribed. Those bundles of joy seem so precious (and they are). However, I've told folks that the hospitals should be required to put a large safety-orange colored sticker on the side of every bassinet with these words boldly printed: "WARNING! HANDLE AT YOUR OWN RISK! THE CONTENTS OF THIS MAY MAKE YOU FEEL MORE VULNERABLE THAN ANYTHING ELSE IN THE ENTIRE UNIVERSE! THEY WILL MAKE YOU FEEL HELPLESS! BEWARE!"

If you think I'm kidding, then remember back to your first trip to the emergency room with your injured child. I remember Tom's first visit. He was somewhere around three or four. While visiting at a friend's house he fell and hit his head against the dreaded coffee table in their living room. The fall resulted in the classic gash above the eye. He was lying on the emergency room table, screaming in terror while they prepared to stitch him up. I felt like a crazy man. I just wanted someone to cut me instead of him. I felt helpless. Welcome to the world of parental vulnerability. That's one of the reasons emergency-room staff try to get parents out of the treatment room. Parents can be very unhelpful when they feel helpless. We all can be unhelpful when we feel helpless, even in relationships other than the one between parent and child.

When I was new to parish ministry, I served three small churches. I found myself visiting parishioners in hospitals very frequently. Some folks were not that difficult to visit. If they were there for surgery or an acute attack of some illness, it didn't bother me to visit. I knew they were going through a temporary, difficult time in their lives but soon would recover and return to everyday living.

Visiting other parishioners in more critical situations terrified me. They never knew it, but I was really, really scared. If someone was dying, terminally ill, or suffering from some terrible trauma, I felt incredibly helpless. What was I supposed to say? What was I supposed to do? I knew I was the pastor and was supposed to be able to help, but I didn't feel very helpful. How could I be helpful in the face of such conditions?

The terror I was experiencing resulted in my pacing up and down the hospital corridors, sometimes passing a parishioner's room several times before I garnered the courage to enter. Then I had a brainstorm! I figured out that if I went into the hospital room and held the parishioner's hand that would help prevent me from running away. The parishioner probably thought I was trying to be warm and fuzzy. The truth is, I was holding their hand just to keep from bolting out the door. I was still so afraid of my helplessness.

I have had several men say to me over the years, "I don't know how you do it. I don't know how you go into those hospital rooms and places like that when people are sick and dying. I couldn't do it." I think back to my days of pacing in the hallways and know exactly what they mean. Feeling helpless hits all of us really hard, but I think men are even worse about it. I think we have the ability to get to the "insanity" place from the helpless feeling much faster than most women.

It's when men or women feel vulnerable that we are capable of the worst. When we feel helpless we can be pushed to do some of the most insanely unhelpful things, or to do nothing when something is required. Our vulnerability scares us to death . . . "and fear leads to anger, and anger leads to hate, and hate leads to suffering," and so on, and so on.

I can't begin to tell you all of the hurtful stories I've heard in my office that would not have resulted in such pain if parents had pushed through their anger to confront their fear. When families have come to me for help, it's not uncommon that they engaged in many hurtful verbal and sometimes physical struggles at home by the time they walked into my office. When the symptoms of the depression start to emerge as defiance and other disrespectful or disruptive behaviors, the parents often get "hooked" by their fear and counter with more force.

In a way, it's perfectly understandable. The parents are afraid they are losing control, so they apply more force to try and regain it. The parental response is understandable, but not really helpful. The continued application of force in difficult moments will probably result only in more pain and suffering, even violence. When parents and their teens gain more understanding about the illness, confront their fear, and try new approaches other than the more reactive ones, healing begins to occur. One mother described her and her husband's journey toward healing with their severely depressed child in a note to me. She said they found along the way "hope where there was chaos, knowledge where there was violence." Even when the depression itself is not showing much progress toward lifting, changing the way we relate with each other as parent and teen can bring about great relief.

When we face our fear, when we face our helplessness, we become open to the presence of God, and the healing hope God's Spirit has to offer. As I stood in those hospital rooms holding my parishioners' hands back in the early days, I gradually learned to offer my fear to God. I gradually learned to admit to God that I felt helpless. As I did that, something began to change. I began to feel God's presence instead of the helplessness that had consumed me. I began to feel God's presence in spite of the pain in the room. That presence I felt was what empowered me to become more genuinely present with my parishioners. That's when they began to tell me how "helpful" it was to have me visit. I wasn't helpless. I was doing something. By the graciousness of God's presence I was being present. I quit pacing the hospital hallways. I quit holding their hands to keep me from running away. I began holding their hands so I could be more present and facilitate God's presence.

When I controlled my anger with Tom, I discovered it was really that old enemy, the fear of helplessness, that was hurting the relationship with my son. Then I was finally able to reconnect with what I learned in those hospital rooms near the beginning of Tom's life. I did not know what was going to happen to Tom. I did not know if he would graduate from high school. I did not know a lot of things, but I did know that if I were faithful to being present, life would be okay. We would be okay. That's what I felt, so that's what I tried to do. I could feel God being faithfully present with me, so I could be present with Tom. Then I could hear God's Spirit saying to me, "Just keep loving him."

Don't get me wrong. It didn't happen in a moment. Even after I came to this new awareness, there were still times when something would happen with Tom and I would feel myself starting to get angry or really scared. After Tom began to recover, I still had a few setbacks.

Sometimes a difficult situation would happen with Tom, and I could see the despair flash across his face. My heart would sink. The knot would start to form in my stomach. However, then I knew to stop and ask myself, "Wait a minute, what am I afraid of?" I would follow the thought and find that it was often an irrational fear fueled by something other than the reality of the moment. Maybe it was a gnawing memory about my own life or my past. Maybe it was something about other teens I had worked with in difficult situations. Maybe I just felt helpless, and the feeling was quickly trying to hide in the anger. I could always get back on track by stopping and asking myself, "What am I afraid of?" I continue the habit to this day. If I find myself getting worked up about something, whether it involves family or other areas of my life, I stop and ask, "What am I afraid of?"

Sometimes when I "slipped," God would have to remind me to be careful and focused. One night I had just fallen asleep and the phone rang. It was Tom. This was later in the journey, when he had started to recover, but could still slide easily back into the hole. He had a job, a car, and a girlfriend. He had driven her home that evening after getting off work. It was shortly after midnight when his car conked out on the interstate. He was calling for help.

Now, I'm no different from the rest of you. I was awakened from a sound sleep. I had to get up for work early the next morning. I was pretty annoyed, frustrated—okay, angry. I jerked my clothes on, seething with each button and zipper, almost savoring the bad mood I was in. I went out to my truck and headed down the road for the "rescue," grumbling and muttering all the while.

Earlier that day I had been listening to a tape of Handel's *Messiah* on the truck stereo. I had left the stereo on when I stopped the engine, so the tape automatically picked up when I headed down the road to find Tom. I got a couple of blocks up the street, still fuming, without really hearing the music. Then suddenly, the lyrics of the masterpiece taken from Isaiah 9:6 pierced through the fog of my frustration: "unto us a child is born, unto us a son is given." I knew instantly God was talking to me. The anger rolled away like water off my hiking boots, and I was reminded of the privilege I had been given. My son, the child I had been given, needed help . . . and he called me. A teenager needed help, and he called his father. What a privilege for that father. I almost missed it. By the grace of God, when I reached Tom, I was ready to be helpful, not hurtful.

Many things emerged from this "awakening" that Patti and I experienced, two in particular that I want to mention here. First, it helped us see Tom more clearly. The more present we could be, the more we could see the intricacies of his struggle. We learned to read him much better. We learned to watch the illness rise and fall. We learned to see Tom's courageous efforts in the fight against the illness.

We began to see more clearly that Tom was not passively enduring all of this, playing into it, or trying to use it to his advantage. He was fighting it. We could see that he was trying to cooperate when he felt like it. I don't mean, "felt like it" in the sense of whether he wanted to or not, whether it suited his plans or not. I mean he went along with things when he felt less of the impact of the illness. We could see him trying some of the suggestions we were making.

One day we had a discussion about things that might help him get to school. We talked about jumping out of the bed at the last minute, heading for the shower, getting dressed and heading out the door as quickly as possible. The idea was to cut the time from bed to school to a minimum. That way it wouldn't leave those extra moments in the bed to agonize about whether or not he could get to school. We wanted to give the anxiety less time to percolate. We also talked about playing some music that would pump him up and help him feel more energized.

The next morning I heard his alarm, then waves of Van Halen pounding against the walls, then the pipes pulsating as he entered the shower, then the shower turning off, then silence . . . and more silence . . . and more silence. I went downstairs to his room and found him fully dressed, standing in the middle of his floor. His head hung low as he mumbled, "I just can't do it," and climbed back into bed. He was desperately trying. I could see it better that morning than before when my anger blinded me. Patti and I used our new awareness to help us roll with the disappointments. It also helped us be more creative and try to anticipate what might be more and less helpful.

Second, the "awakening" helped us take the risks that became so important in Tom's journey. Many times in the weeks that melted into months that melted into years, we were faced with situations that required us to do what we believed would be most helpful for Tom. Some of those decisions required us to do things we never imagined would be part of our family's life plan or way of doing things. Some of the decisions went against what society might have deemed the "right" thing. A few of the decisions went against the advice of others. Some of the decisions broke the rules, even the rule of law.

I guess we broke the law when we let Tom work at a job when he couldn't go to school and was trying home schooling. The job was helpful because it enabled him to leave his dark room and rebuild some self-esteem. Technically, it was against the law for him to have the job if he wasn't in school. I don't mean that we "broke the law" by locking him in a closet, beating him, or doing anything else that would have otherwise hurt him. God's Spirit said, "Just keep loving him," so we took a lot of risks and tried to do the most loving thing in the various situations.

The typical response to fear is to want to find relief from it. That in and of itself is a pretty healthy reaction, as long as we examine the fear and our situation closely enough. If we don't, then our more impulsive, reactive responses can lead us down the path of destruction. Fear is the method maniacal leaders use to control groups and turn them into mobs capable of almost anything, even self-destruction. The fear of the unknown is one of the worst. We hate it so much we will do almost anything to avoid it. This fear is behind some of the worst atrocities in the history of humanity.

Fear evokes a tendency to try to over-control. Driving instructors warn students not to overcompensate in their steering if the tire falls off the edge of the road or the car starts to go into a skid. The idea is to remain as calm as possible and avoid the tendency to turn the wheel too sharply. Reacting too much only makes the situation worse.

Remember the last time you played tug-of-war and you felt the rope start to slip through your hands? You felt afraid that you might lose the game. What did you do? You gripped the rope even tighter and dug in your heels even deeper. It's a pretty natural response. It may work in tug-of-war, but it can be dangerous in parenting a teen fighting depression. Parents should beware of "gripping" tighter when their teen's illness becomes frightening. Gripping tighter has a tendency to push the teen further away.

Frightened people are dying for someone to be the "expert" and give them the answers they crave. The would-be "disciples" want the expert to tell them she or he can see the way into the future. They want the expert to tell them the puzzle can be solved if they follow very strictly prescribed rules. Fear of the unknown will cause us to cling to rules that may at times be hurtful. We hold steadfastly to the rule as long as it helps us avoid facing the unknown, never questioning whether our practice causes more harm than good. It's not easy to say, "I don't know." It's actually easier to say, "Everything will be fine if I only follow the rules."

I've seen some pretty hurtful things happen to people because someone believed the rule of law as prescribed by a literal interpretation of the Bible had to be followed at all cost. I remember a woman who came into my office so scared that she wouldn't even give me her name. She had been severely beaten by her husband on several occasions. She went to her pastor for help before she came to see me. The pastor told her that the law of God dictated in the Bible said she was to be obedient to her husband. According to the pastor's instructions, she was to go home and be a better wife. If she did that, the pastor said, her husband wouldn't beat her. The woman needed support, but the pastor's use of literally defined biblical law drove her back into her living hell. She was in my office because the beatings continued after she returned home and tried to follow her pastor's advice.

I also remember a young woman who told me that she became pregnant as a teen. She was a great teen, very well behaved and active in her church. She attended the church's private school as well. Upon finding she was pregnant, she was forced to leave her home, her church, and her school. Just when she needed the most support, the adults around her used the law to drive her into the wilderness. They were terrified by her crisis and let their fear become the vehicle that drove her away. I've listened to similar stories from others.

We did our best to do what we felt was right and helpful for Tom. We tried to be faithful to love, faithful to God's love as we learned it from Scripture, tradition, reason, and experience. Our faith tradition taught us to use these four gifts of God (scripture, tradition, reason, and experience) as a means for finding our way in the face of fear and uncertainty.

When fear began to rear its ugly presence, and I began to wonder what people might think of us, or wonder whether some particular decision would turn out to be a mistake, I tried to remind myself that God doesn't ask us to be perfect, only faithful. With that thought, I remembered my mother's words from childhood, "Just ask God to help you do your best." It all seemed to come together. God just wanted us to do our best as parents. That's what it meant to be faithful. It was so simple, but not easy.

I also learned in that process that all of my decisions are a little right and a little wrong. Ten years from now a decision I make today may turn out to be the best one I've ever made. Conversely, the same decision ten years from now has the potential for being the worst I've ever made. How can I know the future? I can't. I can only be faithful in the moment. I can only ask God to help me do the best that I am able, and let God's grace handle the rest.

This awareness of God's grace frees me as a parent from the agony of feeling that whatever decision I make today has got to be the perfect one. It frees me from the fear of feeling that this decision will either make or break my child's life. Don't misunderstand. I am charged as a parent with being as careful as possible, to be as engaged in the decision making as possible, to be as concerned as necessary. I'm not charged with being all knowing of the future or perfect in my assessment of situations. I am charged with being faithful. I'm told to do my best. What a relief, and what a difference it makes in the relationship with the teen to live in the awareness of God's grace.

The Gospel of Mark records two encounters between Jesus and the keepers of the law that point to the radical nature of the love required in the kingdom of God. These stories were helpful as Patti and I took our risks with Tom. In the first encounter Jesus' disciples broke the law by gathering and eating grain on the Sabbath. When confronted by the Pharisees, Jesus said, "The Sabbath was made for the good of man; man was not made for the Sabbath" (Mark 2:27). In the second, Jesus broke the law by healing a man's paralyzed hand on the Sabbath. The Gospel says that this act resulted in the Pharisees' meeting with members of Herod's party in order to make plans to kill Jesus (Mark 3:1–6).

The law had strict regulations for what could and could not happen on the Sabbath. Jesus broke the law not once, but twice. His actions led to the plans to have him killed. Was he preaching revolution? Maybe in a sense he was preaching revolution but only because in these situations he simply recognized that hungry people needed to eat and that a paralyzed man needed healing, regardless of the day of the week. The "rules of loving" in the kingdom of God superseded the law as its keepers interpreted it. If that is "revolutionary," then so be it. Parents of depressed teens must be careful their fear does not drive them to become like the Pharisees in the Gospel's account. The kingdom of God requires radical, maybe even revolutionary forms of loving.

As Tom slipped deeper and deeper into the black hole of depression, and we unsuccessfully tried one thing after another, Patti and I took our first big risk. He was about halfway through his first year of high school (ninth grade) and was missing more days than he was attending. Finally, we approached him and said, "Look, our plan is not working. We don't seem to know what will help get you to school. You tell us what you think you need to get back to school. What is your plan?"

That was a big breakthrough for us. We learned to risk asking Tom what his plan was for getting on with his life, instead of telling him what it was supposed to be. It sounds simple, but it wasn't easy. A couple of days later, Tom came back to us with his plan. When we heard it, we were flabbergasted. I never would have proposed anything so bold. I never would have suggested such a risk. It was his plan, so we agreed to take the risk with him.

Tom proposed that he withdraw from high school and return to middle school, where he would repeat the rest of the year in the eighth grade. He figured it would give him what he called a "running start" into high school the next year. Now remember, I already told you that Tom completed the eighth grade with honor roll marks and was inducted into the National Junior Honor Society. I couldn't imagine how he could face the embarrassment of going back. I couldn't imagine that the school system would let him do such a thing. I had never heard of such a proposal (and neither had the schools when we approached them with the plan).

I began this book by telling you it was the story of one of the most courageous young men I have ever known. Tom's plan for getting on with school is only one example of that. Believe me, after I sorted out my anger and fear in the initial stages of the illness and eventually calmed down, I could see what courage it took for the daily struggle through this illness.

Every morning I more or less just get out of the bed, stumble to the kitchen for my coffee, and start off the day. With time and a clearer head, I actually could start to see what agony each morning brought for Tom. Every day was a new reminder of the darkness that enveloped him. Throughout each day there were more reminders of what the illness had stolen from him. Patti and I were able to see all of this more clearly, once our eyes were opened.

I remember going to elementary school with young children who were "held back." It was awful for them. They were mercilessly picked on. Many of them suffered terribly at the hands of their classmates. With those memories, I went with Tom to the high school and middle school to present his plan. I wish I could have photographed the faces of the school officials. They were dumbfounded. I think they were so shocked by the radical nature of the plan that they must have sensed Tom's sincerity in presenting it. Both schools agreed, and the transfer was made. For a while, it seemed to help. Tom made it to school more days. Eventually, the boost from the new plan began to wear off. Once again Tom's absences began to accumulate. We finished the year, but not with much confidence about how it would impact a new start in high school.

Before I tell more of Tom's story and some of the risks, I need to share something important. Nothing ever "cured" Tom. We never found anything that made the illness go away while Tom was a teen. We found lots of things that were helpful for a while, but nothing that became the "magical fix" we so desperately wanted for him. As I've already mentioned, we also discovered lots of things that were hurtful, and tried not to do or repeat them. The journey was one of experimentation. Little by little, Tom found ways to recover.

In a sense, that's another way to summarize the risk taking. We learned to parent by loving experimentation. We approached the situations understanding that we did not know what would and would not work. We could only try something, observe the results, and then use those results to help formulate the next experiment. We might discover something that would work one week, try the same thing at a later time, only to discover that it wouldn't work on the next occasion. We realized we weren't expected as parents to "have all the answers" to every situation. We were only expected to parent by faithful, loving experimentation. Once again, it took some of the pressure off to think and act that way. Thank God for grace.

As the modern version of the Hippocratic oath said, it is important to not be ashamed of saying, "I don't know," and to ask for help. Patti and I asked for help from a variety of sources. We shared our situation with our extended family, friends, colleagues, and professionals in the fields of education, psychology, and psychiatry. Most of the time they just listened and tried to be supportive of Tom and us. Sometimes they offered advice. On many occasions we followed the advice. Once in a while we chose not to follow it. Sometimes our hearts told us it just wasn't right for Tom, so we took the risk and traveled a different path.

Tom's struggle with the school system lasted four years. School became a huge weight upon his shoulders that pinned him to the ground (or in this case, his bed). It seemed there was nothing else that could happen in his life until this "school thing" was settled. Sometimes the school wondered if we were pushing him hard enough. Sometimes they wondered if he should be sent to the alternative school.

At the time when Tom was struggling through high school, the alternative school was the place the school system sent troubled teens that had been removed from other schools because of violence and similar difficulties. The students of the alternative school tended to be more "hardened" teens, many of whom had already been through the juvenile court system and labeled as "behavior problems."

We knew that Tom would be eaten alive by such an environment. It would have sent his anxiety through the ceiling. In spite of his behavior at home, we knew that Tom didn't belong with teens that already had disciplinary problems in the school system, since this was so far from the issue for Tom. We resisted the school's suggestions to send him to the alternative school. The school system had a place for teens that had gotten into trouble. The system didn't know what to do with a teen like Tom who had such emotional difficulties but hadn't gotten into trouble and was so well liked by all his teachers and peers.

The school and others also suggested that we send Tom away to a military school or some other rigid environment like a boarding school. We thought carefully about the option. As a matter of fact, it was very tempting. It would have removed Tom from our house and saved Patti, Rebekah, and me from the daily grind of living with the illness that was torturing us all. It was very, very tempting. Every day was difficult for several years. Every new day meant trying to figure out how Tom was feeling and what he might or might not be capable of that day. Each morning meant Patti and I were "on duty" for another twenty-four solid hours, or so it seemed. It was almost impossible to get a break.

I'll admit we were tempted to send him away to a boarding school or an extended treatment program. Sending him away also might have momentarily given us some relief from our helplessness. After all, if we sent him away to school, at least we could say we had done "something." However, as we watched Tom struggle, we knew that the kind of pressure a rigidly structured system would apply to try and motivate him would probably have had the opposite result.

Tom wanted to comply. He wanted to go to school, he just couldn't. Had more pressure been applied, it probably would have made him feel more ashamed that he couldn't comply and follow the routine. It likely would have driven him further into despair and desperation. Patti and I took the risk, and chose to help him follow his own plan for completing his education and getting that monkey off his back. Some sort of boarding school might be an option for other troubled teens. We just didn't see it as the right option for our situation.

Tom tried several plans to complete his education. We tried to modify his schedule at school on several different occasions. That worked for a while then failed. Next we tried "homebound" instruction. The psychiatrist determined for the school system that Tom was ill and not able to attend school for a period of time. The school arranged for a teacher to come to the house and provide instruction. That was a risk, because it meant we were giving up on Tom getting to school, at least for a period of several weeks. We knew Tom needed socialization with his peers. Staying at home meant he was more isolated from them, but at least he would complete the necessary work to avoid failing and being left behind by his friends the next year. Homebound instruction worked for a while then also failed.

Later we tried "home school." This was even riskier in terms of the isolation. Our experiment with home schooling was several years ago, before home schooling was popular for older teens. It meant that we had to remove Tom from the school system and find a curriculum that we could work on at home. There were very few materials available. We found a self-paced curriculum that seemed to be the best fit. It worked for a very little while then failed just like the other educational schemes preceding it.

At this point, Tom made another very courageous decision about his education. We continued to follow his plan. One day he decided that he would not seek a diploma but rather the G. E. D. This announcement came with mixed feelings for us. In one sense, it brought the possibility of relief from some of the worst part of the struggle for several years. The school "monkey" would finally be off his back. He could close that "chapter" and move on. The educational system had simply not worked for Tom. On the other hand, the announcement evoked a lot of sadness and loss. Tom would not graduate with a diploma. He would not graduate and walk across the stage with his friends.

Even then, we had to continue to take risks as we wrestled with the school system. In those days, the law would not allow a student to take the G. E. D. until the class they would have graduated with had actually graduated. Tom made his decision early in what would have been his senior year. Now what? The school system said he had to enroll in G. E. D. prep classes, so we enrolled him. He went to a few classes, but just couldn't sit in the classroom.

Everyone told us the G. E. D. was very difficult. Tom took some practice tests in the class and passed them all with flying colors. When he failed to show up for class after that, the teacher called and said he would have to report Tom if he continued to be absent. We explained Tom's situation and asked why he needed the class if he could pass all the tests. The teacher was polite, but hung up without our knowing if we might yet have to face the truancy system with Tom.

By this time we had also discovered through our experimentation that having a job really helped Tom. The job was getting him out of the house and helping him to feel better about himself. However, the law applied several restrictions such as the particular hours during the day and the total number of hours per week that he could work because he was supposed to be in school. We helped Tom figure out some ways to do what was most helpful for him. Some of our choices were unconventional. We even might have broken a few laws, but what's one more risk when you're fighting for the life of someone you love?

We managed to hold the educational and legal system off Tom until his class graduated and he was allowed to take the G. E. D. True to his plan, Tom went as soon as possible and took the exam. He passed the exam on the first try. The report said he ranked in the upper percentiles of the class in which he would have graduated. It was a huge weight lifted from him. We could see him change after that chapter of his life had been closed. I know he could have passed that exam much earlier. I only wish the system would have let him take it then. It would have saved him many months of torture.

As Tom's depression deepened, and extended its stay from weeks, to months, to years, our need to take more risks also increased. Patti and I found ourselves making many decisions that we never would have guessed we would have made. Some of the decisions were radically different than what we had hoped and planned for our son's future. So far I've talked mainly about changes that had to be made regarding educational goals. There were also other areas of Tom's life that required rethinking and reassessment of our original plans and goals.

Tom's depression reached a point where he felt so bad that we could barely get him to move. Movement is very important when fighting depression. I tell folks that when it comes to depression, the laws of physics apply. An object at rest tends to remain at rest. An object in motion tends to remain in motion. That's why we tell people to keep moving as much as possible when they're fighting this battle with depression. Once a depressed person sits down, it's hard for them to get up and go again.

Around the time Tom turned sixteen, we were in some of the darkest times. He would barely leave his room. We could rarely get him to do something fun with us. He would not even go and get his driver's license. Can you imagine, a sixteen-year-old male who didn't want his driver's license? (Actually, he wanted it very badly. His illness wouldn't let him go get it.) We figured that if he got his license, he might get out more. Our plan, like most parents' plans, was that his grades would get him the good-student discount on the car insurance, and he could share one of the family vehicles.

With Tom in such a desperate situation, we decided our original plan had to be thrown out the window. We told him grades didn't matter. It was his health and life that concerned us the most. We wanted him to just go and take the driving course out of school (which also meant it would cost us more) and get his driver's license. Even that didn't work, so we moved on to plan B.

Now, plan B was even more radical, so much so that it might shock a lot of you. We took Tom car shopping. We let him pick out a used vehicle. Patti and I purchased the car and parked it in the driveway. "Get your license," we said, "and it's yours." At first, even that took awhile, but eventually he was able to get his license. The whole car-buying affair was one of those risks that made us wonder how others might judge us. I figured that people must have thought we were crazy giving a car to a teen when he wasn't even going to school. Then I heard the voice repeating, "Just keep loving him."

Another risk also involved a car and the possibilities it presented for Tom's healing and development. Remember the incident I described earlier about Tom's car breaking down on the interstate? That incident involved this same car we had purchased for Tom. Although the incident initially provided insight and healing for me as I drove to meet Tom on the interstate, it didn't have a happy ending for Tom and his first car.

After hooking up with Tom alongside the interstate, we had the car towed back to our house. A mobile mechanic came by to look at it the next afternoon. The mechanic surveyed the damage and gave me the bad news. He said the car would need a new engine. It wasn't Tom's fault. It was just the car's time. I knew the car wasn't worth a new engine, so I told the mechanic we'd rather dispose of the car.

As the mechanic climbed into his truck to leave, I looked toward our house and saw Tom sitting on the front porch. He'd heard the mechanic pronounce the death of his beloved car. I could see the cloud start to move over Tom's face. He was about to fall into the well of deep darkness, helplessness, and hopelessness.

This car really had become a major vehicle for Tom's healing. I literally could see his thought process as I watched his face. It wasn't simply, "Oh, my car is gone. I'll have to work to get a new one." No, that would have been more the thought process of someone who was not afflicted by the depression. For Tom, the thoughts I watched unfold were more like, "My car is gone. My life just went flashing in front of my eyes. See, nothing works. I tried. Nothing will ever work. Why bother to try anymore?" I walked over and tried to encourage him. I didn't like what I saw happening to him. He was rapidly tumbling down the well into despair.

It was time for another risk, this time financial as well. Patti and I talked it over. The next day I went to a car dealership and found the cheapest commuter car that any manufacturer produced at the time. I bought it, took it home, and handed Tom the keys to my truck, saying, "The truck is yours to use. When I need it, I'll ask to borrow it. Mom and I are proud of you. We're happy for the progress you're making. We want you to keep going." The first car we bought for Tom was a financial stretch. The second was an even greater leap of faith. Again, as I wondered just how crazy people thought I'd become, I heard the voice inside me say, "Just keep loving him."

Tom continued to improve. He got progressively better jobs, until eventually, he asked about buying his own brand-new vehicle. Patti and I cosigned a bank loan for him to purchase his own new Jeep, taking another risk in Tom's continuing work and recovery. He took a lot of pride in it and in himself. He was faithful with his payments. We never had to make a payment for him. We were beginning to see more light.

Other risks involved some of Tom's activities. When he was seventeen and driving my truck, he was still fairly limited in his activities. He went to work and played a little organized baseball, but that was about it. We kept looking, hoping, and praying for more things to interest Tom and help in his recovery. Be ready to risk when your prayers are answered.

By this time Tom had developed his love for music. One day he came to Patti and me and asked to attend a concert that was in a city four hours away. Some of his friends from across the street had recently moved to that city and were inviting him to attend the concert with them.

Our first thought was, "Of course not! You've never driven that far, let alone driven that far without us. We're worried about your safety, and besides, there's the school thing. If you're too sick to attend high school at this time, how do we justify letting you drive four hours to a concert?"

As we thought more about his request, we began to consider it from a different light. Tom's anxiety and depression had caused him to miss so much of the normal teen events. Frequently it paralyzed him and made it difficult for him to try almost anything new or unfamiliar. Now, he was asking to embark upon an adventure. This was a huge step for him. Part of me was having difficulties believing he was even willing to attempt it.

What a giant step Tom was willing to try and asking permission to attempt! Why shouldn't Patti and I get behind his effort and act of faith? We did. He made the trip and had a great time. Patti and I sat on pins and needles, awaiting his return and wondering if we had done the right thing (and wondering what others thought our "crazy" score was by this point). Through it all, the same comforting voice kept urging, "Just keep loving him."

There were other risks in the journey that are harder to describe, because they aren't tied to particular events. They're more the kind that happened in some of the day-to-day living. For example, we let Tom "get away with" saying things to us that I never dreamed I'd let a child say. Don't get me wrong and think we let everything slide. Patti and I had our limits, but there were many occasions when we just let something slide, like cross words Tom might sling at us in the midst of an exchange.

For example, if he reacted to something in a conversation by making a disrespectful comment and storming off to his room, we didn't chase him down and punish him for his response. Patti and I grew to understand that in those situations, it was the illness, the depression talking, not the real Tom. There was no need for us to prove in that moment that we were in control or could win the fight. Later when he was feeling better, Patti and I would talk with Tom about the incident and any relevant issues.

Believe me, it's a huge risk for a parent to let go of the idea that he or she always has to "win." On many occasions I knew I let Tom say or do things that I would have paid dearly for if I had said them when I was growing up. If things had been different, if the monsters hadn't been in the house, Tom would have paid a similar price. Actually, if the monsters hadn't been on his back, he never would have said or done the hurtful things in the first place. It wasn't Tom talking in those hurtful moments. It was *it*, the life-sucking illness called depression.

I really want to emphasize the need for the parent to back off when their teen goes into one of these altered states of agitation or rage. These altered states often result in the teen saying and doing things they probably wouldn't do if the monster weren't on their back. Obviously, the parents and teen should avoid getting to that particular state of emotional disaster.

If you're talking to a depressed teen and you start to see agitation, stop. Don't press harder. The more you press in that moment, the more you risk an even more intense and irrational response from the teen as the illness takes over. Instead, back off and give them a chance to lower their defenses. Look for another way or another time to approach the subject of discussion. Stop and ask yourself if this is really an issue that needs to be addressed. Maybe it's even time for one of those risks I've mentioned the parent will have to take. Maybe there's some other way around the issue. Try to be creative as a parent, not just confrontational.

Sometimes even when you do your best as a parent to avoid the agitation and rage, it still rears its ugly head. Remember the three fastballs Tom threw down the hallway? Sometimes the rage simply can come out of the blue with very little warning. When that happens, the teen is in what I call an "altered state," and no longer capable of very much rational decision-making and behavior. The teen will continue to believe they are perfectly rational and press forward as long as the parent will engage them. The teen in the altered state will say and do things you never imagined possible.

Many adults and teens that have experienced these altered states have told me that after they calm down there are big parts of the series of events that they do not remember. This experience is where the phrase, "blind rage" gets its origin. People often think the person who displayed the rage is making excuses when they say they can't remember parts of the encounter. Actually, the enraged person is usually telling the truth.

You cannot debate or really negotiate very much with someone who is in one of these altered states. You certainly won't get very far trying to counter them with more of your own force. Countering with more force is likely to set off an even more explosively dangerous outburst on the part of the teen in an altered state of mind. All the parent really can do in the moment is to try and help the teen get out of the altered state. Forget everything else. There is nothing else that can be argued or resolved in the moment. Just back off and help the teen calm down. Later, when it's clear that the teen is calm, rational dialogue and negotiating can occur.

This sounds fairly simple, but it's another one of those things that's not as easy as it seems. When you're the parent face-to-face with a raging child that just said or did something very hurtful or disrespectful, it's very difficult to remain calm and resist the urge to show them who's the boss. Parents, if you are still having trouble believing this, then try this example.

Have you ever tried to talk with someone who was drunk? Alcohol intoxication creates another one of these altered states of consciousness. It seems like the more the person drinks, the more convinced they are of their rational abilities. If you need proof, ask yourself this. When is it easier to get the car keys from someone—before they start drinking, or after they start drinking? If you've ever tried it, then you know that the answer is before. As the alcohol starts to work on the brain and send the person into an altered state of consciousness, it inflates their sense of self-confidence. The more they drink, the more confident they are in their ability to drive a car. If that's not an irrational thought, then I don't know what is!

When I was a young pastor starting out in the parish, I used to get phone calls late at night from people who had been drinking. I'm not sure why, but for some reason they decided after they were drunk that they needed to bend the pastor's ear. At first I tried listening very patiently and offering whatever advice seemed appropriate. Then I realized they weren't really hearing anything I was offering. They were just going on and on. They could almost sound logical and rational, but they really weren't. They certainly thought they were rational and made a lot of sense because they kept going on and on and on and on.

After a while I caught on. I learned to recognize that these folks were in an altered state of consciousness. They weren't really talking with me. They were just talking at me. They really couldn't use any help I could offer them over the phone while they were in their alcohol-induced altered state of consciousness. Instead of letting them pull me into lengthy conversations, I learned to politely tell them that it was evident that they had been drinking. Because of that, they really weren't in a very good state of mind to be talking with me. I would be happy to talk with them in the morning in my office. They would usually try to talk me out of my conviction, but I would end the conversation and politely hang up the phone.

That's all parents can do when their son or daughter is caught in an altered state of agitation or rage. Just end the conversation. Sometimes the agitated teen will continue to pursue the argument and even follow the parents from room to room. Simply and calmly stand your ground. Refuse to debate or argue while the teen is upset. Encourage the teen to do whatever they've found that calms them, but don't let them pull you back into the debate. I know I've hit this issue pretty hard, but it's very important. Let's move on. We were talking about risks that Patti and I found necessary to take in walking the journey with Tom.

As Tom began to recover and get out more, his sleep cycle tended to stay tilted toward the opposite of ours. Consequently, he liked to work late shifts and go out to eat afterwards with his co-workers. That meant another risk for his worried parents. It meant we had to get used to the idea of going to sleep while Tom was still out of the house. We kept an eye out and were ninety-nine percent certain there were no unhealthy things going on like drugs or alcohol, but it still was a risk. We allowed him to stay out later than we would have liked, since these were chances for him to socialize with some co-workers and feel affirmed in his work. It also meant he was out after the county curfew for teens. We were willing to take the risk with him and explain to the county, if necessary. Again, the voice was pushing and comforting with, "Just keep loving him."

I've saved for last the biggest stretch for Patti and me. This one turned up the volume the most on the speaker that was blaring in my ear, "What will people think?" We wrestled over and over again with questions like, "What will my parents think?" (Patti's parents had both died by this point.) "Are we doing the right thing? What will happen if word gets out? Will people understand? How will we help Rebekah understand?" It feels like it's a risk even now to write about our decision. At the time it seemed to be the most helpful and loving thing to do, so we risked it. With time we've seen that it was the best decision. When we made the choice I was guided by the same voice (the voice I believe to be the loving Spirit of God) once again saying, "Just keep loving him."

At some point in his recovery Tom began to work at the ice rink not far from our home. It was a great place for him. He was good at his work and was well liked by his peers, supervisors, and the patrons of the rink. The management even gave him a chance to deejay during some of the public skating sessions and discovered his incredible talents for public speaking, relating with others, and entertaining.

One day well into his recovery, Tom was working at the ice rink when he met a girl his age named Monica. They struck up a relationship, and that was the start of something wonderful and healing for both of them. Tom and Monica each had their own burdens, so in addition to their friendship, they became each other's "counselor" and support. They seemed able to help each other recognize things that were difficult for each to see on their own. They were able to confront and support one another about appropriate and necessary changes that were needed in each other's lives. Patti and I watched as they began to mature together. We began seeing a lot of Monica around our home, and suspected she and Tom were falling in love.

I woke up early one morning and discovered that Monica had spent the night at our home. I was pretty upset. These were not the values that we raised our children with, and neither Tom nor Monica had asked for our permission. She just spent the night. I was also surprised, because I trusted both of them. We knew they loved being together and were so good for one another's healing, but this was not what we had expected.

At first we thought this was one of those "fights" we needed to win, but later changed our minds. It seems Monica's home was becoming a difficult place for her to live. Changes were taking place there that made her feel like she had to get out. She and Tom were determined to be together. They were both eighteen by this time. It was clear that if Patti and I didn't take a risk by allowing her to move in, the two of them would try to start out on their own. We knew they were not ready for that. We did what love required us to do, even though it seemed highly unconventional and unexpected. We invited her to stay.

Thus began yet another chapter in this amazing experiment with Tom. We wanted to give Tom and Monica the opportunity to mature more and make decisions about their futures either together or apart. We tried to be supportive, without pushing them together or apart. In later years Tom and Monica have told us that their time with us was very important in their relationship. They watched how Patti and I lived and loved in our marriage, and gained understanding for their life together as a couple. I never set out to mentor my son and future daughter-in-law in that way, but it turned out to be a good experience for them.

Patti and I also had to work with our daughter, Rebekah, to help her understand that this situation with Monica living with us was not what we expected or really wanted. It was not something we would choose or advise for our children. Basically Rebekah said, "Don't worry mom and dad. I get it." She's pretty amazing, Tom's little sister. Rebekah and Monica have become for one another the sisters that neither had growing up as well as good friends.

While Tom and Monica lived with us, Tom continued his successful climb up through the retail industry. He eventually entered the management level and was given his own store. Monica held down a job and put herself through college at the same time. They worked hard, saved their money, and began thinking about plans for their relationship far into the future.

One day Monica slyly flashed her hand to show us the ring. Tom and Monica were married in September of 2004, and bought their first house together at the end of that same year. The wedding and move into their own home was one grand celebration that we were privileged to be part of. In many ways, the wedding was the result of a lot of hard work, prayerful risk-taking, and listening on all our parts. The voice had been right all along when it kept whispering, "Just keep loving them."

Once upon a time there was a son who went to his father and asked for his inheritance so he could leave his home and family and strike out on his own. Reluctantly, the father gave it to him and said good bye, not knowing if he would ever see his son again. After squandering all of his money, the son was destitute and needed help. He decided to return to his father's home, hoping the father would at least accept him as a servant. When the father saw him returning, he joyously welcomed his son and ordered a celebration. Not everyone reacted to the son's return with the same jubilation of the father. Others, including the father's older son, were puzzled and couldn't figure out why the father would "reward" such bad behavior from his son. The father rejoiced because he thought his son was lost forever. What else matters when you have back the loved one you thought you'd never see again?

Many of you recognize this story as a rough paraphrase of "The Prodigal Son," a parable told by Jesus and recorded in the Bible (Luke 15:11–32). Jesus shared the parable with his followers to alert them about the radical perspective change they would need to faithfully live in the kingdom of God. The kingdom of God requires that we see the ones we love through the eyes of a parent who knows the child can be lost, even lost forever, without a second chance. Living with this sense of vulnerability helps us see more clearly the precious nature of life, the gift that God bestows upon us and trusts us to nurture. Knowing all of this can give us the perspective change we need in the Kingdom. This new perspective of the Kingdom causes us to see everything in a different light and guide our decisions about our lives and the lives of the loved ones we have been entrusted by God.

I've had many couples in my office that have spent a lot of time telling me how they hurt each other when they're outside my office. Sometimes I've told them that I was tempted to send them for "cemetery therapy." That usually gets their attention, so I explain: "Cemetery therapy" means you go to the cemetery together and watch a family bring the body of their loved one to a hole in the ground and leave it there. After everyone has left, you go and stand beside the grave together, stare down into the hole, and imagine that it's your partner you've just placed there."

Most people have gotten the point pretty quickly. Maybe we wouldn't hurt our loved ones so much if we remembered we might lose them so easily without a word of warning. I'm the drummer for a Christian rock group called, I. N. O. A. I wrote the lyrics for one of our songs and based them on the story of the prodigal son. I called the song, "A Father's View." Here's the last verse:

> "Now what would it mean for each of us here,
>   If we thought we could lose one another?
> Would we chew on them less, and cherish them more,
>   If we thought they'd be gone by tomorrow?
>
> For the God of Grace keeps showing us,
>   We're valued in just the same way.
> 'You're precious to me," God says to us,
>   "And that's how to treat one another.'"[4]

Tom didn't leave home like the prodigal son, but his illness took him away from us in many other ways. Patti, Rebekah, and I were constantly aware we might lose him for good. Living in that reality changed our perspective and gave us a much clearer view of the kind of radical love Jesus said was demanded in the Kingdom of God. I still hear God's Spirit urging, "Just keep loving them." You see, there really is light in the darkness.

---

4. Nelson and Johnson, "A Father's View."

4

How Do We Sing a Song
to the Lord (in a Foreign Land?)

Exploring the Spiritual Dimensions of Depression

"By the rivers of Babylon we sat down;
there we wept when we remembered Zion.
On the willows near by we hung up our harps.
Those who captured us told us to sing;
They told us to entertain them;
'Sing us a song about Zion.'
How can we sing a song to the Lord
in a foreign land?"

(Psalm 137:1–4)

WHEN THE Israelites were defeated in battle and sent into exile by their captors, it posed terrible hardships for them. They were torn from their homes as well as their lands and means of survival. Many of their family members and friends also were taken from them. The pain and suffering must have been almost unbearable, resulting in a tremendous spiritual crisis. Where was God in all of the hardship? Why had all these terrible things happened to them? If ever they were to know wholeness and happiness again, they would have to find their way back to more than their homeland. They would also have to find their way back to God. They would have to develop a new relationship with God that could also embrace them in their suffering.

When depression drives its victims into what can feel like emotional exile, it also poses a spiritual crisis similar to the one faced by the exiled Israelites of the Old Testament. There are many aspects of a person's life that must be given attention in the fight against depression. In the rest of this book I'll speak more to those various dimensions. I want to begin that effort by emphasizing the spiritual dynamics involved. Like the Israelites, the depressed teen exiled in the land of despair may need a new way of relating to God in order to find the promise of hope.

As Tom fell deeper into his depression, he eventually reached the point that he quit going to church. Up until that point he had been very active in the life of the church. One of his last activities in the church was to go through confirmation class and accept for himself the blessings of God in Christ that his parents had affirmed at his baptism. Tom chose to be confirmed in the formal liturgy of the United Methodist Church and become a full member. Shortly after his confirmation, the depression started to pull him under, and he pretty much disappeared from events at the church.

We encouraged Tom to try to attend worship and participate in the church's youth group. I even took him on a few mission trips with the youth group from our church. He worked hard on the house repairs we were assigned but had difficulty connecting with the rest of the group. He and I usually wound up hanging out together during the group's free time. As I watched Tom in those times with the other youth, I continued to be amazed by his attempts to break through everything that was happening to him. Most of the time there just didn't seem to be much progress in spite of his hard work.

When Tom gave up on church, I wasn't surprised. It must have become pretty difficult for him to be part of the church when he felt so bad. I'm not really sure, because Tom was pretty quiet about everything. It was really hard to get much out of him throughout most of the journey. Even the counselor we took him to see had the same experience when it came to trying to get Tom to open up. Since Tom so rarely let us know what he was experiencing, we were left pretty much in the dark about his relationships with God or anyone.

After he quit going to church, I wondered if Tom had much of a spiritual life during the tough times. I was surprised during one of our "room cleanings" to find his Bible under his pillow. It told me again how hard he was fighting the illness, and how much he was searching for answers. It also gave me hope that even in his most difficult and "distant" times, he still held on to the values we had taught him and tried to model in our family life.

Parents, if you have consistently taught and modeled for your children faith, self-respect, and respect for others, then in most cases your children will remember these values and build on them in their developmental process. There may be times in the journey when it looks like the child is struggling against some of those teachings and even struggling against us as parents or grandparents. What the depressed teens are really doing is trying out our teachings and giving them a road test. They're also working through a normal process of separating from us and becoming their own person. On the other end of the journey you're likely to find your teen has adapted and embodied much of your faith and values. Parents, the process may not look exactly like what you envisioned, but try to have faith about your child's ability to embrace and incorporate the faith and core values that you have lived with them.

Our vision as parents includes the sight of our children sitting next to us as we worship together. Unfortunately, our normal or typical experience of church worship can become difficult for teens and adults who are depressed. First, church worship may start to feel the same for the teen as school—boring. Even though I'm a preacher, I'm willing to admit we've all sat through some pretty boring sermons and church services. I know I've been guilty of preaching a few myself. However, if you recall, we're not talking about that more typical sense of being so bored by the sermon you plan the next three weeks' evening menus while you're waiting for it to end. We're talking about the same difficulty in connecting with what's going on around the depressed teen that makes them feel disconnected in school or worship; it's what we call "zoned out."

Interacting with people is another factor that can make it difficult for a depressed teen to be in church. If people know the depressed person is going through a tough time, they're likely to ask a simple caring question like, "How are you?" Even that simple inquiry may feel like sandpaper being rubbed over the skin of the depressed teen. The fact that the depressed person can't answer the question truthfully (or even at all) can make it feel incredibly frustrating for them. The depression even can make its prisoner feel guilty and shameful because they can't seem to connect with those around them.

Sometimes it is more uncomfortable and difficult to feel alone in a room full of caring people than when one is actually lonely because there's no one else in the room. If the depression is hidden, and no one suspects anything is wrong, sitting with others can intensify the feeling of isolation. The situation can also create tremendous pressure and anxiety about "keeping up the act of looking fine" to those around the depressed teen or adult. These reactions and feelings experienced by the depressed person are some of the things that may contribute to their deciding to stay away from church, school, and other community activities.

Of course, if a person can handle being in a worshipping congregation, it may provide them with support for their spiritual life and the support of a prayerful and caring group of people. The paradox is that at this difficult time in the depressed person's life when church and prayer are so necessary, connecting to God and to one's spiritual community can be tremendously painful and difficult.

I encourage depressed people to attend the church of their choice, and try to educate them about how to try and make it work for them. When we see them in church, we should rejoice with them, but not pressure them to "feel okay." It may be all they can do simply to be there, even though they feel awful. They may be feeling exactly like the exiles in Psalm 137. They may feel like they're exiled in a foreign land, and asking them to sing songs of praise might seem like a cruel joke.

I know I sound pretty adamant about this, but it's really important. It can be incredibly frustrating for the depressed person when people around are pressuring them to feel better. The frustration can lead to the individual feeling more like a failure. It's like heaping more weight upon the crushing load they are already carrying. The pressure to "feel better" becomes another reminder of their failures. You want them to feel better, they want to feel better, but they don't. "See, I've failed again," they say to themselves. They may react to this sort of pressure with anger and push further away. Then they may feel worse because they acted that way . . . and the cycle goes round and round, getting worse all the time. The author of Proverbs seemed keenly aware of this dilemma when he wrote, "Singing to a person who is depressed is like taking off a person's clothes on a cold day or like rubbing salt in a wound" (Proverbs 25:20).

Most depressed people who walk into my office are convinced they are weak individuals. They're convinced their problem is more a flaw in their personality than anything else. They think they're weak because they have so much difficulty doing what seems to come so easily for others. They're convinced they're weak because they can't accomplish a lot of the day-to-day tasks they used to be able to perform. Moreover, they're convinced they're weak because they ought to be able to do things to feel better. Finally, add to that mix the unhealthy things they might have done in an effort to feel better (like drinking, over-eating, etc.) and it's easy to see why they think they're so weak.

Depressed people are often convinced that they are spiritually weak because they may be having so much difficulty feeling God's presence. They even may think they're spiritually weak because it feels like their prayers asking God to help them find healing are going unanswered. "If I really had faith, wouldn't my prayers be answered?" they wonder. Maybe they hear that same message in their church. I have had several clients over the years tell me that, unfortunately, that's exactly the message they've heard in their place of worship. If that's the message, then what else can the depressed teen or adult conclude other than the fact that they're a spiritual failure?

I always make it a point to explain to folks fighting depression how strong they really are compared to the rest of us. They're not weak! By the time they drag themselves into a counselor's office, they've already made a valiant struggle through the valley of the shadow of death on their own. As I'm working with these clients, I ask them to consider life like a footrace. They are running it just like the rest of us, except they run while carrying a fifty-pound weight in their arms. They're not weak. I try to help them to see that it's amazing how much they are able to "run" while "holding" or fighting a burden the rest of us don't carry and may not even see in them.

Depressed teens and adults often struggle spiritually because the theology they've been given doesn't quite work in the situation in which they find themselves. The depressed individual may be experiencing the most severe spiritual crisis of her or his life. The big *why* stares them in the face. "Why is this happening to me? Why is God punishing me like this? If it's not punishment, then why is God allowing this? Why isn't my faith strong enough to make it go away?"

Young children think in very concrete terms. Here's an example of this kind of thinking from a story that's recently been making its rounds on the computer Internet. A mother and her young daughter were walking on the beach at the ocean and came upon a dead seagull. The daughter asked, "Mommy, what's wrong with the bird?" The mother replied, "Well dear, the seagull died and went to be with God in heaven." The little girl thought a moment and asked, "Then what's wrong? Why is it still here? Did God throw it back?"

We explain life to young children in very black-and-white terms with little room for gray. "Good" cowboys wear white hats and "bad" cowboys wear black hats. It follows then that when we teach children about life, and help them develop their spiritual relationship with God, we use simple, concrete terms and ideas they can understand. When young children ask where God is, we tell them that God is in heaven. When they ask where heaven is, we tell them that heaven is "up there," in the sky. Those are the kinds of concrete terms they find meaningful and helpful. However, when a child becomes an adult, sometimes the "childlike" faith they've originally been taught has not expanded enough yet to adequately address the more complex questions they face in their lives.

Another example of this dilemma can be found in a story that comes from the early days of the space race between the United States and the Soviet Union. A Soviet cosmonaut concluded that God must not exist, because as he circled above the earth in the space we would normally consider "up there," he could not see God. If one can travel "up there" in the sky and not find heaven or God, then the explanation we've been given as children fails us. When a child's concept of God meets a challenge such as the cosmonaut's inability to "find" heaven or God anywhere in space, the child can feel as if their faith stories are nothing more than fairy tales. As a child matures, we need to help them make the transition to a faith that will also help them with the complexity of life they've become exposed to as teens and adults.

As an adult you may laugh when you read the account of this cosmonaut because we know that heaven is not floating a few hundred miles above the surface of the earth. As we've gotten older and more spiritually mature, we've come to understand that "up there" is simply a concrete way to describe something that totally defies any human attempt to describe it. Understanding heaven and God requires a leap of faith into the unknown. Because we can't explain this to a young child, we tell them heaven is "up there." We tell them that their grandmother who just died is "up there in heaven with God." That's what comforts the concrete-thinking child. As an adult with a faith that has hopefully matured beyond the concrete, you draw comfort from knowing that your departed parent is in heaven with God. However, you're not really staring at the clouds to see which one grandmother's literally riding.

There is a spiritual translation that is necessary as we pass from childhood into adulthood. We must take the spiritual tools we were given as children and translate them into a theology that will work with our adult awareness and reasoning skills. That does not mean that at times we are not childlike in our faith. However, it does mean that in times of suffering and crisis, we must also have the tools of a more mature spirituality to help us through our difficulties.

It is quite a dilemma. We have to teach children in ways they can understand, knowing at the same time that the child will turn into a teen and "grow out of" the tools we have provided. Here's another example of this dilemma. It comes from a radio interview I heard a few months ago.

A father giving the interview explained that he had a young son who was just old enough to understand that something can happen to people resulting in our no longer being able to see them. We call that something, "death." The child didn't really understand the intricacies of death, but did know that when people die, they don't come back to be seen again. Having reached this level of awareness, the child asked his father, "Daddy, are you going to die before I grow up?"

The father described how in the next fleeting moments he wrestled with all the possibilities in his brain. Should he be honest and tell the child that his or the child's premature deaths were a possibility? Should he tell the child sometimes terrible things happen that we can't explain or know ahead of time?

The father knew those kinds of thoughts were too much for his young child to grasp. He also knew the purpose behind the child's question. The son needed reassurance that his father always would be there for him. That was the real issue at hand, not explanations about the possibilities of future tragedies. The father knew his son needed comfort and reassurance at that moment. At that age the child really couldn't fully grasp the idea of the future. The father knew what his son needed and gave him the only answer that would fulfill that need, "Of course, son, I will always be here for you."

As that child grows older, he will reach a point where he realizes that his father told him a lie. The son will know his father can't guarantee that something tragic will not happen and end one or both of their lives before the son is fully grown. The son also will grow to know that his father is not a bold-faced liar. Rather, he is a caring father who is trying to be present for his child and give comfort to him in ways that meet the child's current level of need and understanding. The way the father provides that comfort and the way that father answers his son's questions about life will change as they continue along the journey together.

Thus, the spiritual crisis of depressed teens and adults is often further complicated if they face the tough *why* questions with the "outgrown" theology of their childhoods. For one reason or another, the translation or transition from childlike literal, concrete faith to more mature concepts in their faith has not yet occurred. That concrete, "outgrown" but still intact stage of theological understanding attempts to provide the more concrete answers to all the questions it encounters.

QUESTION:
"Why did this bad thing happen to me?"

"CONCRETE" ANSWER:
"If you're good you're rewarded. If you're bad you're punished."

THEOLOGICAL "CONCRETE" ANSWER #1:
"You did something wrong, so God is punishing you. If you change your ways and be good, God will reward you."

THEOLOGICAL "CONCRETE" ANSWER #2:
"God has a purpose in this. Maybe God is testing you or preparing you for something."

THEOLOGICAL "CONCRETE" ANSWER #3:
"The bad thing happened, so God must not really care about me."

Telling a depressed person walking in the valley of the shadow of death that God must have some purpose in giving or allowing the pain that overwhelms them is probably not helpful, and possibly spiritually harmful. If a person is really depressed, living like an exile in the foreign land called "despair and darkness," and you tell them that God has some purpose for their current state of suffering, they just might tell you and *that* God to leave them alone forever. There's also the possibility that the same "God must have a purpose in this" response could cause the depressed person to become more confused and angry with God because the response would send them searching out the hidden purpose for their crippling pain. All of this searching would be happening at a time when their spiritual energies could be more effectively applied to praying about and focusing on God's tremendous ability to heal, as well as God's never-ending supply of deep, deep compassion for those in suffering.

Reminding a depressed person that God has conquered similar pain in the past and can also conquer their present pain can be much more helpful. Such a reminder can prove helpful if it's offered at the right moment. Remember, timing is everything when you're walking this kind of journey with a depressed person. As with most kinds of healing, the process must progress at it's own pace. Forcing or rushing it can prove more unhelpful than helpful.

In the moment you encounter a depressed person, they may need you to be quiet and simply be with them. They may need you to walk beside them in the valley of the shadow of death without judgment and without offering the many "helpful suggestions," which may have been given and tried before. If you try to deal with your own discomfort in the situation by offering more of the same "suggestions" it may send a subtle message to the depressed person that you're uncomfortable with their pain and just want them to "get over it."

The depressed teen or adult simply may need you to be with them. Don't let your fear drive you to give them the kind of answers that may have comforted them when they were children, but now fall hollow, empty, and possibly hurtful in the midst of their current struggle. It may make you feel less uncomfortable to offer an explanation because it may make you feel less helpless in the moment. Unfortunately, your desire for comfort might cause more discomfort for the depressed person. They simply may need your quiet but helpful presence with them to reassure them of God's presence and hope.

Suffering is not simple, nor is it easily explained. Don't drive the depressed person further into despair or further apart from others they need with answers that no longer work for them as a teen or adult. Depressed teens may need help doing some of the necessary faith translating, which requires the supporting faith community member, friend, pastor, parent, or other family member to face their own fear, walk with them, and help with the translating. Remember, that fear of helplessness we talked about earlier knows its way inside a church door. It can cause us to say and do unhelpful things in the church pew as well as at home. Try not to let your fear interfere in the spiritual journey

As the parent of a very depressed teen, I can remember sitting in church on many occasions and having that same experience of living in exile described by the psalmist. In particular, I remember one very long Advent season that felt like it lasted several years instead of several months.

I was waiting and praying for the promise of new life in the birth of Christ. I knew it would come, but I also knew it probably wouldn't be that particular Christmas Day, or any day soon for that matter. Occasionally, my fear would overtake me momentarily and I would wonder if the day of new life would ever be realized.

Through this experience I developed a whole new appreciation for "waiting." Before this I think I assumed that we ask God for something and wait to experience the fruits of our asking as we receive our expected response. It's sort of like saying that God is in the response. In that kind of scenario we experience the waiting as an insignificant inconvenience, with the real power of God coming in the end result. In this journey with Tom I learned that God was in the waiting, helping Patti and me become more present for Tom. The "waiting time" was important. We learned things in the "waiting time" that were also helpful in the healing.

As a young pastor visiting in those hospital rooms I mentioned earlier, I was asked many, many questions about suffering and pain. The same questions were repeated over and over again by different patients in hospital rooms and other settings. As I began to feel less anxious about needing to have the "right" answer for each person I was encountering, I could allow God's presence to work through me. Part of what I figured out was that I didn't have to figure it out. It's incredibly important to acknowledge that none of us has all the answers. "Why was my son struck by such severe depression and anxiety? Why is there suffering in any particular person's life?" My answer is this: "I don't know." How can I know? Only God knows.

Of course I want to know. It's natural for all of us to want to know the "why's" involved in our own suffering and the suffering of those around us. I want to know so much that I tell people when the day comes that we're all standing in line waiting to get into heaven and talk face to face with God, don't be surprised if you see me pushing to get to the front of the line and ask my questions.

Any effort to explain the "why" is probably just an attempt to deal with the fear of feeling helpless. Since none of us except God can actually explain or know "why," it's best that a person trying to support a depressed teen first deal with his or her own anxiety from having to answer, "I don't know." This first step is critical in order to be present with that teen in their suffering.

Saying, "I don't know," does not mean one is helpless. It is a huge leap of faith for someone to say, "I don't know." Making this leap of faith results in a huge sense of relief. This leap happens by putting our faith in the presence and ongoing work of God's Spirit instead of fighting anxiety by offering empty, shallow platitudes. This act of faith helps us avoid getting in the way of God's possibilities for healing, and helps us stay closer in step with the one who is suffering.

It may not prove helpful for the depressed person to be told, "just ask and it will be given." They've probably already asked more times than anyone can begin to imagine. The afflicted person in this case needs to know there is also a form of faith that has meaning in the midst of the exile. They need a theology that works in the midst of the suffering, not one that can sometimes lead one to believe that suffering is abnormal for people with real faith. They need a theology that helps them walk with God even in the foreign land of clinical depression.

I like to remind people that Psalm 23 does not read, "Yea though I walk through the valley of the shadow of death, I will fear no evil, for I know you have a map for the detour." Comfort comes not from the promise of a detour around the pain, but rather, from the promise of God's presence in the midst of the turmoil. Still, the promises of still waters and green pastures in the psalm bring hope and comfort, but also seem to blunt the real horror of the valley. When we read it, somehow it always feels "nice." Don't get me wrong, that's important at times. We need to hear the assurance that God's miraculous love is always working for comfort and hope. Yet, in the midst of the deepest despair, the "nice" feeling might not always speak to the need of the depressed person.

That's why I like to recommend Psalm 22 to people who are struggling with depression. That particular psalm is certainly not "nice." The author makes no attempt to protect us in his description of the horror of the valley of the shadow of death. We get a very clear picture of the despair experienced. Let's look at one part that's very powerful. It even provides the coaching that therapists using a cognitive approach to fighting depression could admire.

In Psalm 22 the author let's us know how badly isolated he feels in his present situation. He begins with, "My God, my God, why have you abandoned me?" You can't get much clearer than the image created by that lament. This statement of the psalmist also describes the state of despair experienced by the depressed person that we talked about earlier. It is the despair that threatens to make the depressed person forget they've ever felt any different in the past, and helps cement them to the thought that the future can hold only more despair. They think, "It's hopeless now, it's always been hopeless, so how can the future be anything but hopeless. Why bother?" However, the psalmist doesn't leave the reader floundering in the state of despair.

The psalmist manages to break through the despair to remind the reader and his own self that the past was actually very, very different from the present state of suffering. He might not feel the brighter, more hopeful feelings of the past in the present state of affairs, but at least he can remember that it was different in the past. Life wasn't always so awful. He recalls, "It was you who brought me safely through birth, and when I was a baby you kept me safe. I have relied on you since the day I was born, and you have always been my God" (verses 9–10).

With that memory, something important has happened. The psalmist finds permission to feel connected with God, even at the same point that he feels bad and says, "my heart is like melted wax" (verse 14). The presence of his pain does not mean God has abandoned him. The psalmist is not alone in the valley of the shadow of death. He can take great comfort in that awareness even though at times his heart is truly aching.

This awareness and assurance gives the psalmist the confidence to proclaim that he knows the Lord will work in the future the same as the Lord has worked in the past. The psalmist continues, "He does not neglect the poor or ignore their suffering; he does not turn away from them, but answers when they call for help" (verse 24). In the valley of the shadow of death, we are not alone. That cognitive triad of despair that I mentioned before has been broken. The present pain was not always part of the past and therefore is not guaranteed to rule the future. Despair is confronted and negated by hope.

Psalm 22 can also give the depressed teen or adult a model for their own prayer life. Prayers in times of suffering don't have to sound "nice." Maybe that seems like a no-brainer to many, but I have talked with a lot of teens and adults who were afraid to let God know exactly how they felt. They had been taught that sharing their feelings of pain, anguish, doubt, anger and fear was disrespectful and inappropriate. No wonder it was so difficult for them to feel God's presence. They had been taught that God could only hear them if they were "nice."

I don't think that's how the psalmist was praying when he said, "My God, my God, why have you abandoned me?" (Psalm 22:1). I teach people to pray honestly with God, to communicate not just their thoughts, but just as importantly, their feelings. I teach them to pour their souls and guts out if necessary . . . and then listen very carefully.

The trees were finishing their annual proclamation of the majesty of God's creation. The colors in their leaves were fading as fall began to anticipate winter's arrival in the Appalachian countryside. I was that new pastor in my first parish, a couple of years under my belt, with a lot to experience and learn. The youth group from my parish trick-or-treated for UNICEF, had a Halloween party in the church basement, and camped out for the night on the church floor.

One couple from the parish called me early in the evening to ask if I had seen their son, Bobby. He had been home alone that day on a one-day suspension from high school for some minor infraction. He was a good, but probably misunderstood, teen. When the parents returned home from work that evening, they couldn't find him. They wondered if he'd shown up at the party. Unfortunately, none of the youth or adults at our Halloween party had seen him.

I spent the night with the youth and other adult leaders in the church. As usual, it was one of those "no-sleep" sleepovers. Early the next morning, I was indulging myself with a cup of coffee when the phone rang. One of the youth leaders answered and gave me the terse message from Bobby's parents on the other end of the line. The parents had just found Bobby. He was in the woods across the meadow from their house. He was dead. They wanted me to join them as quickly as possible in the woods where they found him.

I raced over the winding country roads to their home. I recall singing "Amazing Grace" at the top of my lungs to maintain my focus enough to keep the car on the highway. I was scared to death but knew I had to pull myself together. Bobby's parents were counting on me.

When I arrived, the mother and father called out to me from the woods. I followed the trail of their voices across the meadow and into the stand of trees. I found them clutching each other, looking down at what seemed at first glance like a department store mannequin tumbled headlong on its side. The arms and legs were stiffly angled in peculiar ways. One hand was frozen in its last gesture, the pulling of the trigger that ended Bobby's life. The small bullet hole in his chest near the heart revealed the secret of his final moments on this earth with us.

Since I was the only one the parents had called, it was imperative that we return to the house and call the sheriff. I went back with them and made the call. The parents became concerned that a hunter or wild animal might wander by and disturb the body. Their home was a good ways from town, so it would take awhile for the sheriff to arrive. I volunteered to go back to the woods while they remained at their home to direct the sheriff to the body.

I felt utterly alone and terrified as I leaned against the tree just a few feet from Bobby's body. Slowly the terror was replaced by a powerful rage that welled up from the core of my soul and demanded that I confront the god that had called me to that place and moment. I began to pray in a way that I had never prayed before. I spat each word through clenched teeth with all the fury and resolve I could muster. "Okay, God, I'll teach these kids, I'll play with these kids, I'll lead these kids, but by God, I will not bury these kids! That's it, I quit!" In that moment I had one of the most honest conversations with God that I had ever had in my life up until that point. I held nothing back and let it rip from the very core of my being.

Suddenly something very strange began to happen. To my great surprise, I began to feel the presence of God. There's no other way to describe it. Instead of my prayer chasing God away, it seemed to signal God to come even closer. It seemed I could feel and hear everything alive in the woods around me. The Spirit of God was walking in those woods with me. I could feel it, and I had the profound sense of standing on sacred ground. I was no longer alone, and I was no longer terrified. Instead, I felt the most powerful sense of peace and assurance. It was that experience that not only kept me in the ministry but also helped me be present with Bobby's family as we walked through the valley of the shadow of death together in the days, weeks, and months that followed.

Our deepest pain requires the most gut-level, honest sort of prayer we can muster. It's the kind of prayer that might startle some people. For depressed teens, it's the kind of prayer that moves those awful feelings something like the music we talked about earlier. The heavy pain of depression may need "heavy" prayer as well as heavy metal music.

The opportunity for God to be present through our patient presence is what the depressed person needs to experience from those who want to be supportive. If the church is to be helpful and faithful, it must be willing to affirm with the depressed teen or adult that suffering does happen. It has happened in the past, and it will happen in the future. The source of the suffering is often a mystery. Sometimes we may be able to connect the dots and see how bad decisions contributed to the suffering, but often we cannot. Just the same, God is present with us and will continue to provide the miracle of life that awakens us all to a new day each and every morning. Maybe not today or tomorrow, but someday, the sun will shine again. In the meantime, we must be God's feet and hands reaching out to those suffering and in need of help. We must hold the hands of those who suffer and walk with them in their darkness.

Depressed people often tell me they don't like to go to church because they can't feel God. They sense that others around them can experience God's presence, but, unfortunately, the depressed person can't feel the presence of the Spirit. I like to remind them of that game we played as kids called, "electricity." We'd hold hands and pass "the charge" around the circle by squeezing the hand of the person next to us while someone tried to follow "the charge" around the circle and guess who had received it.

I encourage depressed folks to think of experiences with their worshipping community something like that childhood game. If you can't feel God's presence in the moment, at least hold the hand of someone who is holding the hand of God. In other words, hold the hand of someone who is feeling "the charge" of God's presence. For awhile, the depressed person may have to settle for the knowledge that even though they can't feel God's touch, the friend who is holding their hand can feel God's hand. Eventually the "charge" will come to the depressed person, and they will feel the warm, comforting sense of their own hand in God's hand.

The Apostle Paul was a man who knew the meaning of pain and suffering. He'd been shipwrecked, thrown out of town, imprisoned, and threatened with death, just to name a few of his more serious situations. When he testified about the power of God's love to hold us through hardships, his words came from experience. As the church and as individual Christians, we must proclaim with our actions the same testimony the Apostle Paul gave in response to his many hardships when he said, "there is nothing in all creation that will be able to separate us from the love of God which is ours through Christ Jesus our Lord" (Romans 8:39).

Positive relationships provide the most important tool in the management of depression, and our relationship with God is number one on the list. The practice of that relationship with God is of the utmost importance for parents and their teens fighting depression. That's why I've devoted this entire chapter to depression and spirituality. When pastoral counselors and other therapists start to talk about things in addition to spirituality that are helpful in the fight against depression, some people of faith get the impression that the role of spirituality is being diminished. I've included an entire chapter on spirituality to help dispel any doubts about the importance of spirituality in the fight against depression.

When teens fight depression, they may or may not find the more corporate, public expressions of religious practice to be helpful. They may need more personal, private ways to engage with God. Don't assume that just because your teen decides to skip church attendance, their spiritual life and relationship with God are no longer important to them. If they are unable to participate in a community of faith, help them find alternatives for study and prayer, and continue to model a life of spiritual discipline for them in the practice of your own faith.

There were many times during Tom's darkest days that I wondered about his spiritual life. He wasn't going to church with us. All Patti and I could do was practice our faith and walk through the valley with him. He rarely shared much about what was going on inside.

I remember in particular one day when Tom went to dinner at a friend's home. This was after the darkest days, when he was well into his recovery but still rarely attending church with us. He came home after the dinner at his friend's house and shared some of the experience with Patti and me. He talked about the food and how it compared with his mother's. (He was quick to confirm that hers was better. I guess he knew which side his bread was buttered on.) He shared a little about some of the other guests. Then my ears perked up when he made one simple statement. He seemed really surprised that "they just all started eating when we sat down at the table. No one even said 'grace.'" (Saying a prayer before meals was one way we had continued to model our faith with Tom.) He had noticed the absence of a prayer at his friend's home. Ah, so his spirituality was important to him. The Spirit often works quietly and mysteriously. Don't panic. Be patient, and just keep loving them.

5

The Hurler, Anaconda, and Grizzly
(and Other Things that Help)

Exploring the Many Other
Dimensions of Depression

IT WAS a beautiful day at the ballpark. Patti and I really enjoyed watching Tom play baseball. That game was the love of his life (before Monica). Tom really was a great baseball player. Patti and I worked hard to keep him involved in the sport. Sometimes my heart would go out for Tom as I watched him play his favorite game and saw how his anxiety was starting to interfere and ruin the game for him.

The coaches knew Tom had a great arm as a pitcher, but the more anxious Tom got, the less accurately he pitched the ball. The worse his performance became, the more anxious he felt. What a vicious cycle! As Patti and I watched from the sideline we could see the wave of self-doubt and doom start to cloud his face and complicate his favorite game.

Tom's anxiety also made it difficult for him to hit a curveball, but it took us a while longer to figure out that part of the equation. Tom was a home run slugger, but throw him a curveball and he'd strike out every time. I remember one evening watching Tom at an all-star team practice. Tom's coach was admiring his swing. They began to pitch curveballs to Tom, and the inevitable happened. He'd swing and miss . . . and miss and miss. The coach wondered if Tom needed eyeglasses. The next day we took him for an eye exam. His vision was perfect. Hmm . . .

I was a musician, not a baseball player, so I couldn't be much help for Tom in his baseball pursuits until one day when a coach explained a curveball to me. It seems the curveball breaks on the way to the plate. In order to hit it, the batter has to hesitate before he swings. The batter momentarily and patiently has to wait to see if the ball is going to make that last-minute break before it reaches the plate. Simply put, Tom's anxiety wouldn't let him wait. He'd swing and miss. After we figured it out, he broke the curve ball slump.

Sometimes I would encourage Tom to practice pitching with me as his catcher. I hoped it would help build his self-confidence and conquer some of his anxiety. He had a killer sinking fastball. It would drop right at the plate and clobber me every time. I wasn't the greatest catcher, so between the sinker and my ineptitude, I had lots of bruises to show for my efforts. I pushed Tom to practice because it was a form of therapy. Sometimes we could get him to play baseball when nothing else even could get him out of the bed.

For a while, Tom and I tried early morning pitching in the field across from our house. We thought it might help him over the morning anxiety hump and make it easier to get to school. Tom would get up at 5:30 in the morning and go over to the field to pitch baseballs to me. He was willing to try a lot of things if we thought they might help. Patti, Tom, and I kept trying different strategies to confront the problem. Patti and I could see how hard Tom was struggling against the monster. He wanted to be in school and living his teen years with his peers instead of spending his days and nights in his room that depression had converted to his prison.

Patti and I had to be careful, even with baseball. A couple of times Tom misunderstood and thought we were pressuring him to be a star baseball player. We were just trying to keep his confidence up so he would continue to play the game. It was something he was good at, and he desperately needed all those kinds of things to help get him through the darkness. The depression and anxiety were working hard to make him doubt everything about himself, including his ability to play baseball.

Now, let's return to the ballpark. On one particular day at the diamond, I was standing at the fence along the third baseline. Tom was playing third base, so I could see the action up close from where I was standing. He was due to bat first when his team finished the inning in the field and went in for their turn at bat. I knew Tom really wanted to bat again before the end of the game.

A big guy from the other team was a runner on second base; he was just dying to make it to third. The batter hit the ball and I watched the play begin to unfold. It seemed almost like slow motion. I could see exactly what was about to happen. The runner was going to slide cleats first into third base and take Tom out. He was going to try to knock Tom on his rear so he could get the base. If the runner succeeded, Tom's fast temper would spark the inevitable fight, Tom and the runner would be ejected from the game, and I'd get to go home early and finish some of the work I'd been putting off in order to watch Tom's games.

The runner slid into third, and Tom went flying to the ground, just as I had predicted. However, that's where the similarity with my prediction ended. The umpire called for time out. Tom got up, stepped away from the base, and brushed himself off. Then he walked over to the fence where I was standing. Looking at me with a mischievous grin he said, "You know, Dad, a year ago I would've beaten the hell out of that guy."

Wow, I was stunned! Tom had just given me a peek inside himself! The ride home was tough. I wanted to ask fifty million questions but knew better. Instead I chewed more holes in my tongue. I got pretty good at biting my tongue. That's another important lesson I learned from Tom. When the window opens and teens want to talk, drop whatever you're doing and listen. When the window slams shut, don't waste your strength (and their patience) trying to pry it open. Believe me, this holds true for most of the teens I've ever met.

What Tom was acknowledging that day at the fence by third base was very important. He was feeling different, better in a sense. The fast temper was gone. Now instead of erupting before he even knew the rage was coming, Tom had a moment to actually think about how he wanted to respond. The intensity of his feelings was also much less.

Tom wanted to stay in the game and bat, so he calmly avoided a confrontation with the runner. Instead of punching the runner, Tom walked over and "poked" some fun with me. What stopped the rush of intense rage and gave Tom back the moment he needed to think about how he wanted to respond? What gave Tom back the moment to choose his own response instead of being driven to respond in an unhealthy way that would have robbed him of his next at-bat? Prozac, an antidepressant medication prescribed by his doctor, gave Tom the moment he needed to react and act like his true self.

The day Tom beat his door down, Patti and I made an appointment to see a psychologist and a psychiatrist. From my work as a pastoral counselor I knew that some form of talk therapy and a medical intervention would both be necessary components of Tom's help and recovery. There are several different kinds of talk therapy and several different kinds of professionals who offer talk therapy. Psychologists, clinical social workers, pastoral counselors, and others all offer various forms of talk therapy.

Patti and I chose a particular therapist for the talk therapy because they had a good reputation for working with teens. This therapist also happened to be a psychologist. We might have chosen a clinical social worker, pastoral counselor, or some other therapist instead of a psychologist if we had known one with as good a reputation as the psychologist we chose. The psychologist met regularly with Tom for talk therapy and also had occasional visits with Patti and me.

People get confused about the difference between a psychologist and a psychiatrist, so I'll offer a brief explanation. A psychologist is basically a counselor who has a doctorate (usually a Ph.D. or some similar degree) in psychology. The psychologist can provide diagnostic testing, talk therapy, or some other specialized part of treatment like biofeedback. Any or all of these services might prove necessary and helpful in a teen's management of depression.

The psychiatrist is a medical doctor (M.D.) who specializes in psychology and psychiatric medicine. The psychiatrist is the professional on the teen's team of helpers who can prescribe medications. Years ago, psychiatrists did a lot of counseling along with prescribing medications. Today, many of them have started to specialize in medication management, prescribing the medications for patients and sending them to counselors for some form of talk therapy.

The psychiatrist gave Tom an antidepressant medication called Prozac. It is a drug in the family of antidepressants commonly known as the SSRI family. The "SSRI" refers to the way the medication works in the brain. There are other families of antidepressants that are also used in the treatment of depression and related illnesses. In addition, there are alternative types of medications such as antiseizure drugs and anti-anxiety drugs that are also used to help teens and adults fighting depression and its relatives.

I'm not going to go into a lot of detail about all the different drugs in this writing. Ask your counselor or psychiatrist a lot of questions about any medications that might be involved in the treatment of the depressed teen. It is really important for parents and the depressed teen to know what positive effect the medications are supposed to yield, how the medications work, and any possible negative side effects the medications might cause. Don't be afraid to ask lots of questions!

Within a couple of weeks after Tom started on the Prozac, the ballistic temper went away. It just left. Tom was able to control himself, and it made our lives at home a lot easier. However, the Prozac didn't help Tom with other symptoms like the fatigue and anxiety that also burdened him. The psychiatrist decided to take him off the Prozac and try a medication from a different family of antidepressants. Within five days after Tom quit taking the Prozac, the temper and irritability returned. The psychiatrist added the Prozac along with the other drug, and the temper faded away once again.

Earlier I said that teens want to make good decisions and be successful. They don't want to hurt others with their temper and irritability. The illness is pushing them. There really is a force pushing the teen to act in hurtful, sometimes irrational ways. If you can introduce a medication and the temper goes away without them even trying, it proves the point.

I've also seen this temper disappearance phenomenon with many adults. I had a married couple come to my office one day and tell me that they were ready to divorce. The wife was tired of her husband going off on her and the children with his ballistic temper. His rage had finally worn her out. She was ready to end the marriage.

After I listened awhile, I suspected that the husband might be suffering from some form of depression. It appeared that the ballistic raging temper was one of his leading symptoms. I suggested that he might want to ask his medical doctor about trying an antidepressant medication to help with the temper and other symptoms. The husband and father really wanted to keep his wife and family, so he agreed to consult his doctor and try an antidepressant medication if his doctor agreed with my assessment.

This connection between the ballistic temper and depression is something we've been learning more about in recent years. It's taken awhile for some professionals to get the news. Frequently I've had people come to me who were sent through anger management programs, but never alerted to the possibility that a ballistic temper could be a symptom of depression. Years ago, there were also family medical doctors who were unaware. When this husband I just mentioned first asked his family doctor for the antidepressant medication, the doctor refused. The doctor told my client that he didn't show enough symptoms of depression to warrant the medication. When the husband told the doctor about my explanation, the doctor relented and gave him the drug.

About three weeks after I first saw the couple, they returned to my office. The wife looked at me and quickly blurted out, "I can't believe it. This is the man I married. He hasn't gone off on me, or the kids. We love him!"

The man excitedly jumped in and added, "Yeah, I haven't done anything different. It's great."

At that moment I caught the look on his wife's face. She was ready to kill him. She thought he meant that nothing had changed. If he thought his behavior over the past few weeks had been the same as before they met me, then she was headed out the door! If that's what the husband meant by his comment, then she was convinced he really didn't understand or admit the suffering he had caused his family. In her mind, there was no more use in trying to repair the marriage. One look on her face screamed the message of doom for the marriage.

The husband also saw the stormy look cross his wife's face and said, "No, wait. I know I've been incredibly different. I haven't gone off on you, the kids, or my employees. I haven't been angry or irritable. I've been amazingly different. What I mean is that I haven't done anything different except take this little pill. I haven't had to work to not go off on you. I haven't had to work to not be angry or irritable. The angry, irritable feelings and rage just haven't been there."

On another occasion a young teen came to see me with her parents. She had a list of all the terrible ways her parents acted toward her. She was frequently angry with them and erupted in ugly, volcanic rage. As I listened to the teen and her parents during the next few sessions, it became apparent that the teen was fighting depression and might also be a candidate for an antidepressant medication along with other interventions. I referred her to her medical doctor who agreed with my assessment and started her on an antidepressant.

The teen began taking the medication and returned to see me a few weeks later. We talked for a while and then I asked, "Tell me more about those things your parents do that really make you angry." She looked puzzled for a moment and then said, "There aren't any." She wasn't kidding or avoiding my question. Remember the sunburn? She wasn't feeling things as intensely as she was before the medication. The medication "took away her sunburn." In other words, the medication helped her brain return to a more typical level of brain chemistry so she was able to shrug off most annoying things. With the help of the antidepressant medication, most of the things about her parents that annoyed her so intensely didn't register anymore.

Let's talk a little more about medications. The whole subject is pretty scary for most parents. I don't blame them. Parents should approach the use of medications for their teen with great caution. Having said that, though, I must add that medications for depression and related illnesses are nothing short of miracles for many teens and adults. I mean it! These medications are another blessing of healing God has provided.

Many times you've heard people pray for God to guide the hands of a surgeon. We recognize that God uses numerous forms of healing, including surgery. Have you ever heard someone pray that God would guide the psychiatrist in prescribing a medication that would be the means for healing? If you have, that's wonderful. However, chances are greater that you haven't heard that sort of prayer. In fact, you may be one who has been told that psychiatry and psychology are "of the devil." We're still slow in acknowledging that depression is a medical illness that also needs God's healing, and that some of God's healing for the depression can come through the work of a skilled physician or counselor.

There is a debate raging today about whether medications should be used to fight depression in teenagers. We need to be very careful in using them; however, I have seen so many lives changed for the better and lives even saved by these drugs, that it's hard for me not to suggest they be used. Sometimes the medications are the only thing that will bring depressed people enough relief to move forward and use other tools helpful in managing the illness.

Here's the illustration I often use to explain the role of medications in fighting these illnesses. There is no pill that will give you the thrill of riding a roller coaster. Trust me, I've had my brain scrambled by many coasters. I've ridden enough of them with my family to know that you don't get the thrill if you don't ride the hill. However, if you're so depressed that you can't get yourself to the amusement park, then you'll never get the positive effects from the roller coaster. You won't get that rush as it whips you upside down and sideways. You won't get that sense of togetherness as you and your friends or family are terrorized by the rocketing, diving, twisting coaster train slamming you around the track.

None of the thrills will happen if you're so depressed you can't get to the park. The medications can give many people the relief necessary to "get to the park." Then you can ride and ride and ride and ride! Wow, you can feel the thrill and celebrate the energy from it! That thrill and energy also help a person feel better. But what if you never made it to the amusement park? In other words, the medications help a lot of people feel better enough to engage in the many other things that are helpful in managing depression. I'll talk about some of those additional helpful things for fighting and managing depression a little later in this chapter.

Antidepressant medications are different from most other medications that are familiar to most of us. Probably the most often asked question involves addiction. Antidepressant medications are not addictive. They are taken differently than most other drugs. If you have a headache, you might take some aspirin and start to feel better in a few minutes. If you have some other sort of pain like a toothache, you might take a stronger type of prescription medication. Again, the pain would start to go away in a few moments. You might have to take the medication again when the first dose wears off, but the effects of the drug are fairly immediate.

Antidepressant drugs don't work that way. If you take one, you probably won't feel any different than you did a few moments before you took the pill. In order for the antidepressant medications to be effective, you must take them every day for several weeks. Only then do you start to feel any relief. It is not uncommon for the physician to have to alter the dosage or try a different medication in order to obtain the desired relief. It's helpful to know that this adjusting of the drugs is fairly common. That way, you're not inclined to give up on them too quickly if they don't begin to work on the first try.

Tom tried the medication path. He faithfully visited the psychiatrist and tried several medications as well as several combinations of medications. The antidepressants had a miraculous effect on the irritability and rage; however, they didn't do much for the rest of his symptoms. Gradually, he gave up on the medications and relied more on some of the other things I'll mention. The medications are worth trying, because for some, they are truly miraculous. However, for others, they may not be of much help.

By the way, before I leave the subject of antidepressant medications, let me tie up one other loose end. Remember the killer anxiety that tore me to shreds every time I stepped in front of an audience or congregation? Eventually I decided to try some Prozac. The anxiety miraculously disappeared. I remember the first workshop I gave at a church after starting to take the medication. I was driving down the road on the way home when suddenly it hit me, "Hey, I wasn't anxious!" I stayed on the drug for about nine months and then discontinued it. The anxiety didn't return. Apparently, that anxiety pathway in my brain that had been reinforced for so many years had finally been interrupted long enough for new, nonanxious pathways to be formed. Several of the antidepressant medications also have very powerful anti-anxiety qualities.

I've often told folks that if the anxiety ever did return, I'd go back to the medication in a heartbeat. It took seventeen years of suffering before I found some relief. I would never put myself through that again knowing that I could get help from a medication. Like I said, the medications work for many, but not everyone. I give thanks to God for my healing.

Let's move on to some other things that are helpful in managing depression. Notice I said, "managing." That's probably the best way to think about the whole process. Part of the counseling with teens and adults fighting the monster is to help them learn to monitor themselves. Sometimes it does feel like the depression just goes away. However, in many cases, living with it involves learning to recognize symptoms and responding with helpful countermeasures. Likewise, it also means thinking ahead and wondering what might be more or less possible given the condition of the teen. The teen has to learn to "take their own emotional temperature," and the parents have to learn to be observant as well.

We learned to watch Tom to see what kind of day he was having. Then we learned to modify our expectations based upon our observation. That doesn't mean we let him manipulate us. It means we accepted the fact that something had a hold on him. Some days he was more "up" and available than others. There were times when it simply was useless to push him to do something when he really didn't feel very well.

Pushing Tom when he was having a bad day would have been like trying to put a square peg in a round hole, plugging a Nintendo game into a Sega system, or pushing wet spaghetti across the floor. None of the efforts would have achieved the desired results, and all of them would have resulted in more frustration for us with resulting damage to our relationship with Tom. However, sometimes in spite of our best efforts to observe and plan, Patti and I were still surprised and made mistakes.

I remember one vacation in particular. We decided to visit New England and stop by the town where we used to live for five years. We'd visited before, and Tom had enjoyed seeing some old friends and stomping grounds. This time proved to be very different. We arrived in the town and watched to our surprise as Tom began to sink into a hole of depression. Patti, Rebekah, and I went out to dinner one evening. We couldn't even get Tom to leave the motel room and go with us. He just couldn't do it. He couldn't face other people.

As Patti, Rebekah, and I talked about our situation over dinner, we made the decision to radically alter our vacation plans. We left town the next morning and planned activities that wouldn't require Tom to "hob-nob" with other people. We found an amusement park on the way home and scrambled our brains on some new roller coasters. Tom still didn't feel great, but he was able to push himself to ride with us. We were thankful for that much.

We were disappointed that we didn't get to keep the appointments with our friends. We were even a little embarrassed as we tried to explain to our friends that we had to change our plans. Rebekah was disappointed she didn't get to spend more time on the beach, but she was able to handle her disappointment because she had begun to understand that changes were necessary at times in order to fight the monster that threatened her brother. We had tried to educate her about the illness. We all knew that changing our plans was the most loving and helpful thing we could do for Tom.

Asking the simple question, "How do I feel?" can be very important for any of us in planning our day's and week's events. We might choose to alter our agenda based on our physical or emotional state of being. Parents asking, "How does my depressed teen feel?" can be just as important. For example, when a teen is fighting depression and having a "down" day, a parent might not want to use that moment to ask the teen to take on a new or especially difficult project. "Do it and do it right now because I want it done right now," is not the best way to approach a depressed teen who's having a bad day.

If you chose not to take on a project on a particular day, it doesn't mean you'll never do it, it just means you might need to delay it until you feel better. Parents need to remind themselves of this as they approach their depressed teen about daily tasks or homework. When people are fighting depression, they actually need permission be more flexible about planning their agenda and taking small, easy steps in accomplishing the necessary tasks they face.

Most of us probably don't stop to realize it, but we generally have an ability to complete a huge task by breaking it down into small, more man-ageable pieces. I remember the time I decided to extend the driveway of our home. I had fifteen tons of gravel dropped at one end of the driveway. The gravel had to be moved and spread over the surface of the new part of the driveway. In case you're having trouble figuring out how much fifteen tons of gravel really is, picture a very large dump truck. Picture it full. Picture it emptying its load at the end of my driveway, with me standing nearby, waiting to move the gravel across my yard with wheelbarrow and shovel. Picture my jaw dropping in shock.

My first thought when I saw the mountain of gravel the truck dumped was, "Are you crazy, Gary? You've really done it this time! You'll never be able to move all this gravel with a wheelbarrow and a shovel!" However, the "you'll never be able to do this," was just a fleeting thought. I started moving the gravel, shovel by shovel, load after load in the wheelbarrow. After I moved several loads over the course of a few hours, I was able to look at the mountain and say to myself, "Okay, I can see it's getting a little smaller. I guess I'll finish it eventually." As I continued to shuttle the gravel in my wheelbarrow, I had to coach myself. I had to keep reminding myself over and over again that the mountain was shrinking. That's how I managed to stay with the task over the next few weeks.

Depression robs the individual of the ability to break something large into smaller, more manageable pieces. The depressed person would have looked at my mountain of gravel and said, "What a mountain! I'll never be able to move that. Why bother?" The "you'll never be able to move that," would have been more than just a fleeting thought for the depressed person. For them it would have felt like an overwhelming, disabling reality. They would have walked away from the gravel pile without filling a single shovel full of gravel.

A depressed person is overwhelmed, not lazy. They lack the ability to look at the larger picture and break it into smaller pieces. That is one of the cognitive changes that come with depression. The depressed teen often needs gentle "coaching" to help them break big tasks into smaller, more manageable pieces until they can regain that ability for themselves.

When you're talking with someone who is depressed, you have to take these cognitive distortions seriously. It may seem perfectly obvious to you that a large task can be accomplished by breaking it into smaller pieces, but it is not so obvious for the depressed teen or adult. They really can't see the situation the same way you see it. The depressed person may not be able to see the solution to a problem even though it seems so obvious to you. Sometimes they might see the same solution but still feel like it's impossible to achieve it.

The depressed person often uses this same distorted vision as they consider their own life and self-worth. They may not be able to see their positive attributes even though those attributes are clearly visible to you. Sometimes all the depressed teen or adult can do is believe that you can see these things about them and will help them through until they can share your view.

It's also easy for depressed people to set themselves up for failure. When a person is depressed, they already feel like a failure, so often they are anxious to succeed at something. They desperately want to find something that will make the pain go away and help them break out of the despair, so they'll often overestimate their ability to accomplish something they think or they're told might be helpful. They have to be warned and given permission to take simple, small steps in order to prevent additional failure and possible despair. Here's an example.

Aerobic exercise can be helpful in managing depression. Walking, running, and swimming are forms of aerobic exercise that get your heart rate up and keep it there for an extended period of time. When I tell a depressed person that exercise is helpful, they often respond by saying, "Yeah, you're right. I need more exercise. I'm going to join the gym." I don't have anything against gyms, but frankly, it probably won't work unless someone else helps them get to the gym. Even then it's doubtful they'll make it.

I discourage the gym approach because it's generally doomed to failure. Here's what I've found generally happens. Maybe the person makes it to the gym every day the first week. However, after that, they go less and less, until one day they say to themselves, "Look at this. I can't even get to the gym every day like I promised myself. Here's one more failure. Why bother to try at all?" Once more they are reminded of what they cannot do instead of what they can do.

A better approach to aerobic exercise might be to start with a simpler alternative. Go for a walk one day. At the end say, "Thanks, God. I was able to walk one day this week. Help me to do it again. " The next week, try to walk two or three days. The next week try to walk three or four days, and so on. In other words, celebrate what you can accomplish instead of grieving your failures. Build on those successes.

Depressed teens need similar encouragement and coaching. They need permission and coaching to approach their recovery with small, easy, manageable steps. As parents who are frightened by the power of the depression our child may be facing, it's easy for us to overwhelm them, even when we're trying to avoid it. We want so desperately for our child to feel better that we can overwhelm them with the best of intentions. Here's an example.

As Tom fell into some of his darkest days and isolated more and more, Patti and I racked our brains to find things that would get him out of his bed and keep him moving in some way. By this time he had shown a keen interest in music but had never wanted to learn to play an instrument. We got the bright idea that maybe he'd like to learn to play a guitar. (My drums were already in the house, but he'd never shown an interest in playing them.) Maybe a guitar would be something he could tinker with by himself and develop some further interest. Maybe it would prove therapeutic and help him feel better about himself.

We were excited by our idea and planned a big surprise for Christmas. We hid the guitar and amplifier until Christmas morning so he wouldn't guess the contents of the packages if we placed them under the tree. When he opened the guitar, he was truly surprised and excited. The guitar seemed like it would be a real hit! Later that afternoon he took it to his room and began to tinker. We included instructional books and tapes with the guitar so he could get a start, and told him we'd arrange for private lessons when he thought he was ready.

At first I heard the twangs and strums of a beginning musician. Ah . . . music to my ears. It was working! He was out of the bed! Then I heard less and less, until finally, nothing. The silence was killing me. Eventually I went to his room and found him in his bed. He was obviously very upset. I asked him what was wrong and got the usual "nothing." We were well enough into the battle with depression, so I had learned to recognize the reaction I was seeing. The guitar completely overwhelmed Tom. The idea of learning to play it seemed totally out of reach. Fortunately, I guessed the problem and asked him if I was right. Tom acknowledged that my guess was accurate.

Patti and I had gotten so caught up in the excitement of our surprise, we never considered learning to play the guitar might overwhelm him. The next day I talked with Tom about the guitar. I could tell it bothered him that he wasn't thrilled with our surprise. Tom knew his mother and I had worked really hard to find something that would help and also please him, so I could tell he sensed our disappointment and felt guilty that the whole idea had failed.

I explained to Tom that his mother and I wanted more than anything for him to feel good. We didn't care if he didn't want the guitar. We were just looking for something that might help. We were willing to return the guitar and get something that might better fit his situation. After some discussion, he and I headed for the music store to return the guitar. I had to keep reassuring him it was okay. It seemed to really bother him that the guitar didn't work for him.

We went from the music store to the electronics store. As we moved from the first store to the next, I could watch Tom start to "lighten." At the electronics store we purchased the latest video game system. Tom already was proficient on a different system. When we got home, he plugged it in, and off he went. I got to watch and cheer. Once again, his plan worked. He really did seem to have a good idea of what might be helpful. We continued to learn to trust that more and more. It really is very easy for depressed teens to be overwhelmed, even when we as supporters offer help with the best of intentions.

Sleep is the next thing for us to look at on the "things that help manage depression" list. Over the past few years I've attended several continuing education workshops dealing with depression and related issues. Every presenter at these events has stressed sleep as one of the major issues in the management of the illness. Depression and sleep make difficult bedfellows. Depression tends to disrupt sleep patterns. For some people, depression makes it more difficult to fall asleep. For others, it makes it difficult to stay asleep, or get back to sleep after they are awakened in the middle of the night. For yet another group, depression keeps them in a more "shallow" sleep, denying them the rest available from "deeper" states of sleep. They may sleep for eight hours and awaken feeling like they never slept at all because they never dropped into the deeper states of rest. The lack of good sleep and resulting fatigue makes the depression worse. It's an awful endless cycle.

I remember arguing with my parents about being allowed to stay up later when I was a teen. I wanted to watch late-night television, read a book, or work on a model. It wasn't simply that I wanted to stay up later because I was older and thought I should have more control of my life. I wanted to stay up later because I was a teen. My body was literally telling me to stay up later. We've learned that teens' body clocks shift, causing them to fall asleep later and awaken later in the morning. This natural tendency to stay up later and sleep later is often amplified by depression and related illnesses.

As Tom's illness progressed, we began to struggle with him at night. We accused him of trying to stay up too late, making it more difficult for him to get up in the morning and make it to school. As we backed off and learned to observe and listen more, we began to notice that he wasn't "trying" to stay up late. His body wouldn't allow him to fall asleep at a more normal time. Patti and I realized that as we were getting tired and winding down for the night, Tom seemed to be winding up.

I've seen this same struggle with lots of teens and their parents. It looks like the teens are trying to stay up, when in fact they can't fall asleep or stay asleep. Many of the teens will tell you that they can't seem to turn their brains off. They try to fall asleep, but thoughts just keep going through their minds. They can't seem to keep themselves from thinking about the intrusive thoughts.

I said before that trust is a critical factor in the fight that teens and their parents wage against depression. Sleep is just another example of the necessity for trust. Parents must trust that their teen is not trying to stay awake. That way they can begin to think of creative ways that might help the teen in the fight to regain a healthy sleep pattern. Likewise, it is critical that the teen is doing his or her best to regain the healthy sleep. If each trusts the other and something doesn't work, the parents and teen can work together to find other options.

A variety of things prove helpful in regaining a healthy sleep pattern. Sometimes music or "white noise" like the sound of a fan can be distracting enough to fall asleep. Morning exercise has proven helpful for some in gaining better sleep, as well as meditation, productive daytime activities, or something as simple as counting sheep. (In today's less pastoral culture, you might wind up counting something like alien invaders from a video game.) The counting process seems to engage another part of the brain and help distract us from the troubling thoughts that keep us awake. In some cases, special medications might also be temporarily helpful to reestablish a healthy sleep pattern. For some, the antidepressant medications also help with the sleep difficulties. Sleep is another area where professional help might be necessary.

Watching television, reading, or other late night activities can also contribute to poor sleep patterns. Be careful about watching the television or even reading late at night. Most of us have a time that we start to feel sleepy. The television is really good at pushing us to fight through that feeling and stay awake to finish the movie or wait for our favorite show.

Have you ever noticed after you fight through the sleepy feeling and finish that movie, you're wide awake, and ready to start the next movie? That's because you ignored your body's cue to go to bed. Your body thought you wanted to stay awake, so it gave you some extra adrenaline, the chemical that "pumps us up" when we need it. You can't sleep until your body has finished processing the adrenaline. Pushing to stay awake long enough to finish the chapter of the book you're reading can result in the same adrenaline dump. Be careful to read your body's cues and turn off the television or put down the book when your body tells you it's time to fall asleep.

Teens, I know you don't want to hear this, but maintaining a regular sleep pattern is really helpful. Teens like to stay up late on some nights and sleep in late on the weekends. Try to go to bed and get up about the same time every day. You might give yourself an extra hour or two on the weekends, but try not to stray too far from your pattern. You can't stay up late several nights and make it up on the weekend. It just doesn't work. Your body needs consistency.

Naps can also be a killer for healthy sleep patterns. Lots of people establish some pretty erratic, unhealthy sleep patterns by alternating inconsistent sleep times with naps. Eventually, they slip into a state of constant fatigue. If you're really tired and feel like you have to take a nap, keep it to no more than thirty minutes. That way you won't throw off your consistent sleep pattern.

Finally, most sleep experts agree that if you don't fall asleep in twenty or thirty minutes, you shouldn't stay in the bed and toss and turn. At some point, your frustration over not falling asleep can trigger one of those adrenaline dumps, which then makes it more difficult to fall asleep. It's better to get out of the bed and do something relaxing until you start to feel sleepy. Then, head back for the bed.

Allowing your teen get up or stay up if necessary in order to take charge of their own healthy sleep pattern requires one of those leaps of faith for parents. It's tough to allow your teen to stay up if their body is telling them it's not time to sleep when you're ready to sleep. Patti and I learned we had to let Tom figure out what worked best for him. Sometimes it felt strange going to bed and knowing he was still up. He managed to figure out the pattern that was best for him so he could do well at his work.

Structure is another factor that is very important in the management of depression. Most of us take for granted that our work, school, or other activities give us a sense of structure to our lives. They give us something to look forward to. The activities give us a reason to get out of bed in the morning. They give us a sense of movement and productivity. They give us a chance to have fellowship with others.

I remember when computer modems first came on the scene and made it possible for some people to work from their homes instead of going to their offices. At first it was celebrated as such a liberating experience. Then, quite a few workers began to experience difficulties accomplishing the tasks required by their employers because the worker missed the structure that going to work at the office provided.

The situation created quite a dilemma and people struggled to find solutions that would allow them to continue to work from their homes. I even saw ads in a magazine for "portable offices." A company would drop a building about the size of a storage shed in your back yard. It was fully furnished as a mini-office. That way you could get up in the morning and have someplace to go outside your home, hopefully re-creating some of the structure missed by working from home. I never heard if the "portable offices" worked. Retirement brings a similar crisis for a lot of folks.

When depression hits and drives teens to isolation, it often robs them of a lot of this kind of structure. Then it becomes even more difficult to get out of bed, because there's no reason to get up. Creating a personal structure can be even more exhausting. The depressed teen often needs help in the planning of activities that might provide some structure. They often need some gentle (I emphasize gentle) pushing. (Remember, parents, sometimes it is necessary to push. Be gentle and careful, and observe the results. Don't keep pushing if it's not working.)

Baseball was one of the ways we tried to provide Tom with structure. Sometimes it worked; sometimes it didn't. There were other things that also worked. Later, Tom developed an interest in hockey and played the sport for a few years.

A hobby I enjoyed for many years became a source of healing structure for Tom. I have to confess here that I am a railroad nut. I always have been, and always will be. My father and I built a very large model train layout in his basement while I was in college. When Tom arrived, my father decided to dismantle the layout, box it up, and send it off with us. Tom and I played with parts of it off and on, but mainly left it boxed in the closet when we moved to Virginia.

One day well into Tom's isolation, a friend of mine who knew of my interest in trains gave me a subscription to a model-railroading magazine. It sparked an idea for me. I asked Tom if he would like to build a model railroad layout in our family room. He seemed to like the idea. With Patti and Rebekah's permission, we took over a large part of the room with the construction of the layout.

There were many days after that when I would find Tom painting model buildings, or casting plaster rocks and constructing them into mountains and cliffs. For a while, it seemed like the railroad was one of the only things we could get him to do. We were happy that it got him out of the bed and kept him moving. It was another way we could see Tom was fighting, and trying some of the suggestions that we were offering. It worked for a while.

Eventually Tom lost interest in the model railroad. It became my hobby, and I expanded the railroad holdings to include an outdoor layout. A few months prior to the start of this book, Tom and Monica bought their own house, complete with a big backyard. One day they were visiting and Monica jokingly prodded Tom, saying, "Did you tell your dad what you're doing in the backyard?" With that sheepish smile that causes me to rejoice every time I see it, Tom said, "Oh yeah, I'm building a railroad."

Patti and I owe a debt of gratitude to the McDonald's restaurant chain. One day shortly after Tom's sixteenth birthday, we decided that a job might be another way to provide some structure in Tom's life. We thought that maybe it would get him out around others his age, give him something to do, and give him some affirmation for a job well done. Patti and I decided to push Tom a little to try this job idea.

Patti took Tom around to several local businesses so he could ask for employment applications. It would have been too overwhelming for Tom to seek the applications on his own. Simply sending him off to get job applications would have resulted in his feeling too overwhelmed and shutting down. He would have felt more failure, and we would have felt more frustration. That's why Patti helped by taking Tom around to the various businesses that hired teens.

We knew how difficult it was for Tom to walk into those places and face the people. His anxiety skyrocketed even considering the idea of trying such a venture. Believe me, it took a lot of courage and teeth gritting on his part to walk in those places of employment. It's hard to fight that voice that constantly screams, "This will never work," when you've heard it for so long about so many different parts of your life. Tom walked into one McDonald's restaurant, and the manager hired him on the spot. A new door toward hope had just been opened.

Tom became a very valued and trusted employee. The management recognized his talents and hard work. They rewarded him with affirmation, free food, more money, and promotions. Although he didn't work there for a long period of time, it helped Tom break through something. It gave him a sense of accomplishment. It helped him feel good about himself at a time when school was doing exactly the opposite. Tom left McDonald's and began the journey to better and better jobs. I truly believe that working those jobs was one of the major sources of help and recovery for him.

I have seen employment provide the same type of help for other depressed teens. You have to remember that school is the major issue in the life of teens. That's the way we set it up for them. If school goes well, it's easier for them to feel good about themselves and their futures. If school is going well, then college might be in the future. That's the next step. They can see it. The future is not some big unknown or void. Knowing that college will follow high school lowers a lot of anxiety about the future.

If school does not go well, where does the teen get that same kind of affirmation? Even if the teen's family is helpful and affirming, the teen is still daily facing that "you're-a-failure" message from school. Besides, even if family is affirming, it's not the same as a boss turning to them and saying, "Hey, you did a great job. I really like having you here. Come back tomorrow," or, "You're doing a great job. I'm giving you a promotion."

If school's not going well, it's hard for the teen to make a connection with the future. If college isn't the next step after high school, then what is? The situation can leave the struggling teen feeling more overwhelmed. Employment is a great source of therapy for a lot of depressed teens because it can provide structure and help them see some possible steps into the future.

Moving on to other things that help, let's talk about the role of counseling and professional help in the management of depression. Be honest. Which would you rather face: the dentist's drill or the counselor's questions? For many of us it's the throbbing agony from a damaged tooth that finally drives us to the dentist's chair. In all too many cases, the dentist just happens to remind us that it probably would not have been such an ordeal if we had sought help earlier.

The same applies to counselors. Parents and teens are reluctant to seek outside help from counselors and usually experience more hurt than necessary because they put off asking for help. There are probably lots of thoughts and feelings that contribute to the feet dragging. I really do understand. Families don't want strangers in their business.

Parents are afraid of what the teens might tell the counselor about them. Teens don't want yet another person asking them, "What's wrong?" Parents feel they know their teen better than a stranger, so what help could the stranger offer? Teens don't want another adult telling them what to do. Parents don't want to feel judged by the counselor. Teens don't think they can trust a stranger with some of their most private thoughts and feelings.

The list could go on. In most cases families probably do put off getting help much later than they should. The result is that more hurt has occurred before they walk into the professional's office. Waiting later rather than sooner to get professional help also allows more time for trust between the parents and their depressed teen to erode.

There are many different forms or "schools" of counseling that are helpful in various situations involving teens and depression. I'm not going to describe them all and give out report cards for results. You could put a hundred counselors in a room and I think you'd get a hundred different opinions. Here, I will simply focus on what my observations and the feedback from those who have walked into my office have reported as helpful. I will say this: I detest "recipes." I am wary when any counselor tells me there is *a* way and they try to force everyone through the same "recipe." (That's a personal beef of mine. Can you tell?)

In the relationships family members share with one another and the relationships they share with a professional counselor, trust is a key factor. When families walk into my office, I know that a lot of trust often has been eroded by the struggle with the illness. I tell the family members that in order to rebuild trust with one another, they might first have to borrow some trust from me. In order to do that, they've got to be able to trust me. I try to be open and honest with the families. I let them know that I will tell them what I know and tell them what I don't know. The most important part of the first meeting with parents and teens is building a sense of trust and relationship.

I mentioned earlier that when Tom's struggle heated up, I began to fear that people would not be able to trust me as a professional. I wondered how parents could feel comfortable bringing their teens to me for help if my own son was going through such difficulties that I couldn't stop from happening to him. It seemed the only thing for me to do was to disclose my situation to parents when they brought their teens to see me. I told them about Tom and what Patti and I were experiencing. Then I told them I understood if they wanted to seek counseling elsewhere.

I was truly amazed by the responses of the parents to whom I disclosed my own painful journey. Every single parent looked at me and said in one form or another that I was exactly the one they wanted as a counselor. If I was going through it myself, then I must really know what they were experiencing. In the years that followed, more and more teens and their parents found their way to my office. Sometimes as I continued to walk in the painful times with Tom I doubted my abilities as a parent and pastoral counselor and wondered if I knew what I was doing in either realm. However, God kept sending more hurting teens and their families my way, so I decided I must have been offering something that was helpful to others. In those times of doubt, it was an act of faith for me to trust that God was teaching me how to be helpful.

I know God didn't cause Tom to suffer through his nightmare, but I will tell you this. Teens and parents who visited my office kept sending other teens and parents to visit my office, so something they found there must have been helpful. I know I could never have been as helpful for other teens and parents if I had not walked this journey myself with Tom. He and God taught me things in that journey I never could have learned in any other way.

Counseling is helpful in different ways, some of which I've alluded to. Sometimes the counselor is the one who hears the pain. The sharing of the pain is important and brings a form of relief and comfort. Often a teen or parent leaves the counselor's office feeling better simply because they feel like someone really listened and understood them. It makes them feel less alone in the struggle.

Another one of the counselor's jobs is to help the teen and parents hear each other more clearly. Parents often enter my office expecting that they will introduce their teen and leave me alone with them. Over time I've learned that teens are not necessarily as anxious for the parent to leave as the parent might think. By keeping them in the room together, it allows the parents to learn more and gain that new perspective about their child and the struggle with depression that I mentioned earlier.

Having the teen and their parents in the counseling room together is similar to what I tell married couples when I work with them. If I sit in the room with one of the members of the couple and listen, the individual doing the sharing builds more trust in me, the counselor, as they tell their story and I listen. However, if I'm in the room with both people and one of them is talking, the trust is also building with the other partner as they hear what is being shared with me. Granted, there are many times when teens need to talk alone with a counselor; however, don't ignore the possibilities that come from the teen and their parents being together in the counseling room.

Sometimes the counselor functions as an educator. He or she explains a lot of the things I've touched on in much greater detail, and helps relate the material to the specifics of each family and teen's situation. The counselor has to educate the depressed teen and those who are part of the teen's family. Sometimes the educating extends to others who might also be part of the teen's support system, such as teachers, pastors, and friends.

Depression is still a huge mystery to most of us. It's important that the counselor help the teen experiencing it to sort out a lot of the more normal thoughts and feelings experienced by most teens from the distortions caused by the illness. That way, the teen can learn to recognize the distorted thoughts and work to replace them with more accurate perceptions of reality.

Actually, the same goes for feelings. When people are depressed, their feelings are also somewhat distorted. For example, when they feel sad, they don't just feel sad. They feel sad and depressed. As the depression lifts and they begin to feel better they have to learn to "re-calibrate feelings". Depressed teens have to learn what "sadness" feels like without the extra intensity from the depression. This is similar with other feelings.

In the case of sadness in particular, there's another important factor to consider. Everyone feels sad from time to time. When a depressed person starts to feel better, and then experiences normal sadness for the first time after that, it can frighten them into thinking that the depression is returning. The counselor has to anticipate some of these experiences for the recovering teen and warn them of what to expect. I tell people I try to stay a step ahead of them in the recovery and warn them of some of the potholes down the road as the journey into healing continues.

Sometimes the counselor is a coach. They help the teen and the parents develop and implement strategies for change. Remember before when

I mentioned that Patti took Tom around to collect employment applications? That's a good example of coaching. Often when I mention that a job might be helpful, a parent will respond with, "Yeah, I told him to go get some applications." What the parent doesn't realize is that the thought of going out, figuring out where to go, and facing the people might seem overwhelming to the depressed teen. The teen is not lazy and reluctant to work. They might really want a job, but can't make their way through the anxiety to get applications. Instead of telling them to go get applications, we might work out a strategy instead where the parent takes the teen to get two or three applications on their way home from the counseling session.

Sometimes the counselor is the one who simply affirms the efforts of teen and parents, even when they're not experiencing the hoped-for results. In other words, the counselor is the one who says, "Look, I know you're really trying. I know you're doing your best. I'm sorry it still hurts, or you're disappointed, but I know you're doing your best."

Peer counseling can prove especially helpful for teens. By *counseling* I mean more than just formal peer counseling programs offered in some schools. I'm also including opportunities for sharing with other teens provided by church youth groups as well as more informal sharing with other teens. It's amazing what teens will say to each other when they won't reveal much of anything to an adult. It's such a powerful feeling to find someone your own age struggling with some of the same thoughts and feelings. Often the teens are able to help each other gain insight and understanding, as well as fellowship and hope. Sometimes it really benefits a hurting teen to reach out to someone else in need. Helping another is a good way to help yourself.

When Tom and Monica met, they each began to share some of their difficulties with one another. In a sense, they became each other's peer counselor as well as friend. Each learned to communicate very private and painful thoughts. They helped each other give voice to things that otherwise might have tortured each of them in isolation. Sometimes they even pushed one another to confront things about themselves that were in need of change. I'm sure this kind of sharing helped pave the way for a deeper relationship that culminated in love and marriage.

When depressed teens stumble into alcohol or other drugs, it requires yet another form of help. Often, they need specialized treatment to deal with the devastating addictions. A professional counselor can help assess the teen and determine the specific kind of help required. Sometimes the teen needs formal addiction treatment programs in addition to other help with the depression. I must add one note here. Unfortunately, I've run into situations where teens (and adults) were admitted into drug and alcohol programs, and the underlying depression was never addressed. That's like treating the symptoms of an illness without addressing the root of the problem. Both the addiction and the depression need treatment. Don't settle for focusing on only one or the other.

This has been a long chapter highlighting some of the things helpful in managing the fight against depression and related illnesses. I've saved the best for last. If you recall, the title of this chapter is, "The Hurler, Anaconda, and Grizzly." By now you might have guessed that these are the names of three roller coasters at an amusement park called King's Dominion, near our home in Virginia.

Tom was about nine years old when we moved from Massachusetts to Virginia. Shortly after our arrival we paid a visit to the amusement park. We had a great day, but discovered that Tom was not interested in trying any of the rides that were very tall. This bothered me, because I've always had a difficulty with heights. I didn't want him to suffer the same problem, so I tried to coax him to ride. He would have nothing of it, so we crossed the park off our list of future family outings.

A few years later, Tom's eighth grade class had a field trip to that same amusement park. They rode the rides and used them as lessons in math and physics. I went along as a chaperone, but tagged along with a different group than Tom. I wondered all day how he would handle with his peers his reluctance to go on many of the taller rides like the roller coasters.

At the end of the day, when I saw him, Tom was beaming! He had ridden all the rides and had a blast! Somehow he had fought through his anxiety and taken the plunge. Patti and I went the next weekend and purchased a family season pass to the park. We continued the practice for the next several years. Since that new beginning, we've scrambled our brains on coasters from Massachusetts to Florida, and Virginia to California.

I'm talking about *play!* Playing with your depressed teen (or any teen) is one of the most important things any parent can do. There is something almost spiritual about play. In the act of playing we forget about our differences, our struggles, our pain, and just play. Don't ask me how to explain it, but there's something truly amazing about play. It gets us outside ourselves for a moment. It distracts us from our obsessions and invites us to simply enjoy being with one another. It's impossible to be upset with each other when you're hurtling down a coaster hill at fifty miles an hour or more and getting flipped and turned so fast you almost black out. You just enjoy the moment—together!

I encourage all parents to learn to play with their children while the children are still young. That way, when the teen years come and they start to say it's not "cool" to be with family, you've got a history of playing together built to stand on. Don't let them fool you. Teens need their parents and family. They will want to be with you if there is something to look forward to. If the family has some playful activity planned, the teen is more likely to want to join in and bring a friend.

Over my years as a counselor I've been amazed at the adults and families that have forgotten how to play. On many occasions I've looked at people sitting across from me in my office and asked, "Tell me, when was the last time that you played together? When was the last time you had fun?" You would be amazed at their responses. Most of them would look at each other with blank expressions, then turn back to me saying, "I don't know. It's been so long I can't remember." How sad for them.

Play is one of the things giving energy to life. Play restores a sense of joy and vitality. Most people tell me they're just too busy to play. Some people think play is "childish" or "irresponsible." You can be playful and responsible! Play increases productivity and creativity. It also helps tremendously with depression.

Too many families set themselves up to fail when it comes to playing together. Here's how it typically happens. They struggle through the week, through all the work, the meetings, the soccer games, and the music lessons. Then, they arrive at the weekend with a list of things they have to accomplish in order to go back to work or school on Monday. They tell themselves that if they finish the list, then they'll take time to play. They rarely, if ever, finish the list, so they never play. Monday starts the grind again, with no sense of joy or rejuvenation.

For people who have forgotten how to play, I give them a simple rule to follow. Play first. You'll still wind up getting as many things accomplished. The things that you don't accomplish are probably not that important anyway and can wait. After my children were grown, I faced a list of things that needed attention around our house. I remember doing some of the chores and thinking, "This is one of those things I set aside to go and play with my kids. This chore could wait, but my children couldn't.

Boy, am I ever glad I got to play with them. Thanks for the blessing, God."

Here's what I offer families as an alternative to the "all work and no play" existence. I tell the family members to take their refrigerator calendar and write down every meeting and event that they have to attend. That includes your children's ball games, dance recitals, and music concerts. Watching your child participate in an activity is very important, but it doesn't qualify as "playing together."

After you've filled in all your events and activities, look at the holes in the calendar. At least once a month, plan a fun event that will be an opportunity for your family to play together. Don't just mark the date and think of something later. I've found that families who do that will get to the date and use the free time to run errands, for example. Fill in an event. That way you're more likely to actually engage in the activity, and you'll have something to look forward to.

It's like Christmas. Half the energy we get from the holiday experience comes from the anticipation. If you mark your calendar like I've suggested, your family will start to excitedly anticipate the next event. You'll know you're getting it right when you finish one event and on the way home your younger child or teen asks, "What are we doing next weekend?"

As a parent you have to be creative about the playing. You might find that the thing your teen enjoys the most is not at the top of your own list. As a parent sometimes you're having fun because the chosen activity is one that brings you great pleasure. Other times you're having fun because you're getting to be with the people you love as they truly enjoy themselves. Parents need to be observant and try to follow some of the interests of their teens. I don't mean that you should try to be one of the teens. That really smacks of insincerity and turns teens off in a hurry. I simply mean that you might have to learn to engage in some of the things that the teens find exciting so that you get to enjoy being with your teen as they have fun doing some of their favorite things.

I am a musician and never really developed a love for sports. Tom grew to love baseball and hockey. We lived near the stadiums for some professional teams, so Patti and I included trips to their games in some of our family outings. Tom taught me to enjoy watching baseball. He helped me understand some of the details of the action that gave me a greater appreciation for the game.

Hockey was a different matter. I still haven't figured it out. I will confess that I even fell asleep at some of the hockey games we attended during the time when Tom was fighting the depression. Tom and Monica recently visited Patti and me during our travels in Arizona. We went to a Coyotes' hockey game together, and once again I had to lean over and ask, "Tom, what's a hat trick?"

I can remember many times during Tom's depression that I would go home after work and ask Tom, "How are the Red Sox doing?" or "How did the Bruins do last night?" To be honest, I really didn't care about the teams, but I knew he did. I knew that following the teams was one of the things that did keep him moving and brought him out of his darkened room. I desperately wanted to stay connected with him. I didn't want him to slip deeper into the darkness and isolation, so I learned to patiently listen as he described the ups and downs of his favorite teams. He was talking to me. That's what really mattered. Years later Tom confessed that sometimes he didn't care about the teams either, but he knew I was looking for some way to connect with him and went along with my efforts.

Roller coasters are another story. That's a passion that our whole family has developed together. I don't know what would have happened if Monica hadn't liked roller coasters. We even got to ride roller coasters with Tom and Monica on their honeymoon! Find a way to play with your teens! I can't emphasize it enough! It's really, really rewarding, and a fun way to just keep loving them!

6

Alligators
(Swim with Caution)

Encouraging Families to Care for Themselves

THE SUN was bright and penetrating with its heat on September 28, 2004. The brilliance of the afternoon made it difficult to believe that only a few days earlier, the destructive winds of a category-three hurricane had lashed this part of Florida yet another time in the same year. The towering oak that lavished us with shade had survived its battle with the storm to witness more of the comings and goings of the many who shared its park.

Spanish moss gracing the elderly oak's branches barely moved on this special afternoon. Tom and Monica stood beneath the boughs of the triumphant oak and pledged their love to each other in holy matrimony. Family members stood nearby in solidarity with them. I was honored and blessed by being asked to perform the ceremony.

The old oak stood close to a tranquil lake. Water nourished the stately tree from the sandy shores of the lake on one side and the marshy ooze of swampland on the other. The narrow neck of glistening beach looked inviting as it stretched from water's edge to the protruding roots of the great oak. I could imagine the beehive of activity normally filling the beaches on a bright sunny day in the middle of summer.

On this special day of matrimonial celebration the beach was empty save for one family lounging in the shade of some nearby trees. Not thirty feet from the trunk of the "wedding oak" was a simple park sign posted on a pole for all to see: "Alligators—Swim With Caution." I had to chuckle when I saw the sign. In a way, it seemed so appropriate for the moment.

Life in a marriage and family is sort of like that. You go to the lake, you see the sign, you figure the warning is for someone else, and you swim anyway. It's only when you're staring at the giant gaping mouth full of pearly whites connected to a piece of floating luggage that you suddenly realize, "Uh, oh! I guess that warning was for me."

When Patti and I started our marriage and family together, we knew bad things could happen. Somehow we were able to put that in the back of our minds, jump in the water, and swim anyway. Actually, that ability to put something potentially dangerous aside is pretty helpful at times. If any of us really knew what trouble faced us in the future, if we thought the warning sign really was for us, we might never get in the water and swim. Even though we came face-to-face with many alligators along the way, I'm sure glad we got in the water and swam. Tom and Monica had already faced more than their share of gators, and certainly would have more to face in the future. Still, I know they're glad they took the plunge.

By the time Tom stood with Monica beneath that old oak, he had fought and beaten many a gator. I guess he could have been called "a slayer of dragons" in days of old. Like many of the struggles in all of our lives, Tom's struggle left him both wounded and gifted. In some ways, the illness he wrestled stole a precious part of his life from him. In other ways it made him stronger and gifted him with more insight, empathy, and maturity.

Really, the illness was like a death for Tom, complete with all the accompanying feelings of sadness, anger, despair, and depression. The monster cost him a lot of his youth. Patti and watched (and knew Tom was watching) as other teens up and down our street went about the business of the "high school years."

The homecoming parade for the high school started in the street in front of our house each year and processed to the school. The parade was full of bantering students representing their school and its various clubs and groups. If you think about it, the parade was sort of a display of lots of the possibilities for students to engage in during their high school years. For Tom, they were more like a procession of impossibilities. Tom never marched in the parade or even watched it from the sidewalk.

When homecoming and prom time came around, the teens living in the neighborhood posed for pictures on their lawns in tuxes and gowns as they headed for the formal dances. Tom never wore a tuxedo or danced. Banners and balloons decorated the houses as families celebrated their teen's graduations. Tom never wore a cap and gown or walked across the stage. Our house remained bare until Rebekah graduated. Tom endured a lot of loss, and yet he fought through it to create a life of his own making.

Imagine what it must take to feel "beaten up inside" and still get out of bed the next day. Imagine what it must take to have your sleep turned upside down by an illness and still make it to work on time. Imagine what it must take to endure the looks and questions like, "Why aren't you in school?" and still walk and work among your peers and adults. Imagine what it must take to miss so much school and still have the nerve to take the GED. Imagine what it must take to watch your friends go on with their lives leaving you behind, and still go out to forge a new life for yourself. Imagine what it must take to feel like every little step requires all the energy you have, and still manage to excel in a sport you love. Imagine what it must take to feel "dead" and still have the courage to live.

Tom can tell you about all this and more. He felt it, he faced it, and he conquered it. Little by little he kept putting one foot in front of the other until his strength returned and his insight, empathy, and maturity increased.

More recently Tom's journey has led him into retail and entertainment management. He has supervised many teens and young adults. Sometimes he talks about his work with me and describes a few of the situations he has encountered. It's very rewarding to hear him describe how maturely he acts, and how he makes decisions with a lot of wisdom for his age. Employers are surprised when they are reminded of his age. They tend to see him as much older.

Tom mentors many of the young people he supervises. He has a deep sense of caring, and tries to be appropriately helpful. He is able to recognize some of his own struggles in a few of them, and sometimes offers part of his story for their consideration. In the past several years he has given me permission to share his story with teens visiting my counseling office. Several of them have gained hope when they've heard how Tom walked in their path of sorrows and found new life.

When a teen has to fight the kind of alligators that Tom faced, the struggle cannot help but have a profound impact on their family. I want to use the rest of this chapter to talk a little more about the care of the family during a crisis like the onslaught of depression for a teen. I've tried to focus so far on things that are helpful to the afflicted teen. Obviously, some of those things are also helpful for the rest of the family. However, I want to give a little more attention to some important factors for those who face the alligators with their teen.

Let's start with the siblings. It's really important that an atmosphere of honesty and openness be established with the siblings of the afflicted teen. This is a delicate process, because the siblings need to know what's going on. However, you don't want it to sound like the parents are talking about the depressed teen behind their back or using the sibling as a sounding board. It helps to frame things in the illness mode. In other words, it's important to talk to the siblings about the illness that is afflicting their depressed brother or sister. Help the siblings understand that a lot of the things you may be doing differently for the depressed teen are necessitated by the illness. You're not giving the afflicted teen "special treatment." You're not "playing favorites." Rather, you are helping the afflicted teen through an illness.

Think of it like this. Maybe you have a rule in your house about restricting junk food so your children will eat the healthy food offered them at mealtime. Maybe sweets are allowed only on a limited basis. Then one of your children gets a really sore throat and can't eat regular food. You might give your child with the sore throat all the Popsicles they can eat just to keep them hydrated and nourished. The other children living in the house might yell, "No fair!" Then you'd have to explain to the siblings that the Popsicles were simply part of taking care of the child with the sore throat. In a sense, it was fair, because you were trying to meet the need of each child. One needed Popsicles to regain strength and health. The other children needed fewer Popsicles so they wouldn't neglect the healthier food served at dinner.

This is not the easiest thing in the world for children to understand (or some adults for that matter). When we're young children, it's perfectly normal that the idea of "fairness" means everyone has the same treatment, or the same toy, or the same amount of something. As each of us grows older, our sense of what is "fair" or "just" needs to change. Somewhere in our development, we need to move to the understanding that things are not always "fair" because they are exactly the same.

If parents go to the ice cream store with a four-year-old and a teenager, the four-year-old will think it's "fair" if everyone gets the same size of ice cream cone. However, if the teen gets three scoops because they can eat it with no problem, but the four-year-old gets one scoop because they'll barely finish one scoop before it melts and hits the ground, you can bet that the four year-old will cry, "That's not fair." As parents we were simply trying to be "fair" by giving both children the amount of ice cream that would be a treat for each.

As we grow older, we hopefully come to realize that "fairness" is more about having needs met than everything being exactly the same. A four year old child doesn't need a triple-decker ice cream cone to feel like it's a real treat. On the other hand, a teen might feel disappointed by a single scoop, so you might get the four-year-old one scoop, the teen three scoops, and try to explain.

Again, I'm not trivializing by using ice cream as the example. It's just easier to make the point. Parents have an ongoing task to help all of their children grow in their understanding of "fairness" or "justice." This teaching process can be severely complicated by the presence of a chronic illness in the home, like depression. Parents might hear the cry, "That's not fair," quite a few times in spite of their best efforts to explain. Given time, experience, and careful support from their parent, the siblings should continue to grow in their understanding of "fairness."

Rebekah is four years younger than Tom, but very early in the difficult journey she knew something was up. She could sense that her parents were struggling. Sometimes she became the brunt of Tom's frustration and anger. There were times when it must have seemed to her like Patti and I were letting Tom "get away" with something.

It was essential that Patti and I explained to Rebekah why we were responding to situations with Tom in some pretty unorthodox ways. We had to help her understand that Tom was afflicted by an illness and that many of our parenting decisions were part of our fight against that illness. She was a very understanding child. Like the story of the interrupted vacation I shared earlier, there were many times when family activities had to be altered because Tom just didn't feel well. That's the way we had to frame it for her. Her brother didn't feel well. If not, it would have looked like we were simply letting Tom set the agenda and manipulate all of us.

As Tom got older, we knew it was safe to leave him alone for brief periods of time. It became important for us to do things with Rebekah, even when Tom refused to join in the family's activities. We had to make sure she didn't suffer too much loss in the process of living through Tom's illness. Recently, Rebekah, Patti, Tom, Monica, and I spent a wonderful day together in Disneyworld's Epcot Center. What a day! Tom was doing some of his clowning with his delightful sense of humor and making the day even more spectacular. Yet, in the midst of it all, memories of a not so wonderful day also visited me.

The memories came from a day years earlier, during some of the darkest times for Tom. The four of us made the trip to Orlando and visited several of the theme parks. On the day we were to visit Epcot Center, Tom announced, "I don't want to go." Rebekah was really looking forward to seeing the aquarium and some of the other attractions in the park. Patti and I looked at each other and made a very difficult decision. We left Tom at the motel for the day and took Rebekah to Epcot. It was an extremely difficult day for us as parents. We worried about Tom but knew we needed to share the park with Rebekah. It's important to keep some sense of normalcy for the siblings.

Rebekah is an incredibly strong young woman who managed to find her way through the troubled waters of her brother's depression. I think the openness we shared with her about the situation helped her discern the path she needed to take that would be different from Tom's. She was and is very self-motivating, which was sometimes hard to believe after the pushing we were forced to try with Tom. Parenting the two children was similar in some ways. We expressed and lived the same values with both. However, in other ways we parented them in a radically different manner. It was important as parents that we remembered that distinction. Once in awhile our anxiety made us forget.

I remember one day standing in our kitchen, listening to Rebekah describe all the schoolwork she had to finish before the week's end. She was in high school at the time. As a concerned parent who had been through many struggles with Tom about unfinished schoolwork, I listened and then foolishly said, "Don't you think you better get started on some of that work tonight?" Without missing a beat, Rebekah snapped back indignantly, "Dad, you don't have to tell me to do my work." I got the point and quickly confessed, "Sorry, Bekah. I was just having a parent moment." Parenting Tom and Rebekah was radically different at times.

The siblings need to understand what is going on for their depressed brother or sister, and they need to understand that parents might have different expectations for each child. However, the siblings also need to be protected from the illness. Sibling rivalry is one thing. Becoming the brunt of the frustration and anger of the depressed teen is another matter. We had to be very careful to protect Rebekah from the frustration the illness was causing Tom. We had to be very firm with him in that arena and make it clear that we would tolerate some things, but we would not tolerate his hurting his sister.

I've encountered this problem in most of the families who have brought me depressed teens. The siblings must be protected. On the other hand, the depressed teen must also be protected from the siblings. It's easy for the depressed teen to become the "fall guy" for the siblings. We didn't face this problem in our family, but I've seen it in many others.

Here's how this particular problem can develop. The sibling starts to realize that the depressed teen has a hair-trigger temper or low tolerance for frustration. The sibling can learn to manipulate the depressed teen in an argument for something the sibling wants by setting off the teen's temper. Because the depressed teen's temper and resulting actions often look like an overreaction to the situation, the depressed teen usually gets in trouble. In the end, the sibling winds up getting what they wanted, because they look like the victim. Working with siblings can be an important part of the healing process for a lot of teens.

Teen depression is a rough road for parents too. You've heard about many of the struggles as we've moved through this narrative. Just managing the daily conflicts and difficulties can be overwhelming for the parents. However, in addition to that struggle parents also experience a loss similar to the one sustained by their depressed teenager. As we moved through high school with Rebekah, every turn along the way was a reminder of what had been stolen from Tom, and in a sense, stolen from us.

Patti and I had a delightful experience as marching band parents when Rebekah played in the high school band. We attended almost all of the football games on Friday nights. We cheered as the band marched in front of our house in the homecoming parades. On Saturdays we followed the band to various competitions. The rest of the season we attended their concerts, helped with the fund-raisers, and dragged the band's equipment from gig to gig.

When it was time for the formal dances, Rebekah and Patti would drag me to all the malls in the area, shopping and shopping and shopping and shopping for formal gowns and accessories. I discovered lots of chairs and benches in women's departments. I could give you a list of the best stores based on the comfort of their "dad's" chairs.

The two of them would get lost in the racks of clothing while I stayed behind with the already accumulated packages. (I learned about the time Rebekah hit the middle-school years that I suddenly lost all sense of what was acceptable garb for a teenage girl. Every time I picked up an item of clothing, I got the "Ugh, not that, Dad," reaction.) Eventually Patti and Rebekah would return from the jungle of clothing and laugh when they found me asleep in one of the "dad's" chairs. We joked that they were "dragging me around." The truth is, I wouldn't have missed it for the world. Patti and I had missed similar adventures with Tom. We never got to see him try on a tuxedo.

As high school neared its end for Rebekah, we began shopping for colleges and anticipating graduation. When the day finally came, we decorated the house with flashing lights, banners, crepe paper, and balloons. Was it gaudy and tacky? You bet! What a thrill it was to see her cross that stage! If it was such a thrill, why was I crying? Were they tears of joy? Of course, but something else also fueled the flow of emotions.

At many of Rebekah's high school events I found myself choking back tears. I was so happy for her! Yet I knew the tears were also part of the grief I was experiencing. My heart ached for Tom as the joyous events of Rebekah's youth reminded me of the torture he had endured. We had all missed so much as he spent those times in darkness.

By the time Rebekah was in high school, Tom had begun to achieve success in the course he had charted for himself. Celebrating his successes made the grief easier. I knew he had missed a lot. I knew that the more traditional path had not worked for him, but there was still a path for him with a fulfilling life to be experienced. Gradually, he was becoming the young man we knew he could be. The alien ship had returned, and released our once-lost son to us. Just watch him go!

Parents also need a lot of care in order to survive the struggle with teen depression. I want to offer some suggestions for the care of adult relationships in these difficult circumstances. I realize that many depressed teens are part of families with only one parent in the home. The suggestions I am offering can apply to married parents living together, as well as separated parents trying to parent together. I once heard years ago that over sixty percent of parents who lose a child to death eventually go on to divorce. It puzzled me at first, but I think I understand it a lot better now. It's very easy for parents to turn on each other when a crisis involves their child.

It's an especially difficult situation for a marriage when both members of a couple face intense pain at the same time. If one of you is going through a tough time but the other is not, then the beauty of having a partnership is that it allows the troubled one to lean a bit on the other. If both are fighting the alligators at the same time, it's hard to lean on each other because you know the other is also hurting.

Maybe you don't want to burden the other parent with your own hurt so you try to hold it inside. That generally makes the pain more destructive for you and widens the gap between you and your partner. If you do try to share your pain, you might find that the other parent is so consumed by their own pain that they respond in unhelpful or hurtful ways. Either way, the gap can widen and threaten the relationship between the parents. In the midst of the kind of loss and pain we were experiencing, it was very important that Patti and I learn to share our pain with each other and not turn our frustrations, pain, and hurt into assaults on each other.

It's difficult to be patient when we are hurting. In some ways we're no different than other animals. Remember how you've been warned to be careful when approaching a hurt animal, be it your family pet or an animal in the wild? The animal's pain causes it to lash out. The same can happen to us when we hurt. Again, if only one partner is hurting, the other might be understanding and patient if the first partner snaps or lashes out in a moment of pain. However, if both are hurting, it's easy for the pain to cause an escalation in the interactions until it becomes an irrational exchange of hurtful comments and accusations. Both parents want someone to take the hurt away, and in a strange sort of way, they feel more frustrated because their partner doesn't seem to be able to do it for them.

It's easy to get to that irrational place. "It's your fault she's acting like this. If you just did it differently, we wouldn't be going through this." What they really mean is, "I don't know what to do. I'm really frightened. Somebody take this pain away." It's critical that parents are very careful with one another at all times, but especially when they're parenting through a crisis involving one of their children. This is not the time to become sloppy and careless in interacting with one another. Remember the basic rule: Don't hurt each other. Maybe that sounds too simple, but it really works.

My caseload as a pastoral counselor has included not only teens and their families but couples struggling with relationships and marriages. I've had many couples stumble into my office, often verbally fighting (and even a few physically) on their way from the car to the waiting room and into the seats facing me in the counseling office. Then they try to show me just how much they can hurt each other by continuing the verbal onslaughts right there in front of me. I don't tolerate much of that abuse. I usually stop them pretty quickly. Both members of the couple want to tell me about all the issues that are making it difficult or impossible for them to be together.

Please don't think I'm oversimplifying things when I say this, but loving someone does not require training as a rocket scientist. I generally stop the fighting in the room, pick up a box of tissues, and offer the following words to the warriors I've just separated. "Now, you might not have fought over which brand of tissues to buy, but you've probably fought over something just about as silly. I can tell that by the way you're going at each other." At that point they both generally nod their heads affirmatively and wait for me to finish, so they can go back to their fighting and efforts to convince me about the negative traits of their partner.

I continue: "Think of it like this. Every time you raise your voice and say something that's hurtful to your partner in order to win the argument over which brand of tissue to buy, you've made a conscious decision. You've decided that this box of tissue is now more important to you than the person you say you love and cherish. I say this because your actions show that you're willing to hurt that person in order to win the fight. You'll hurt each other if it gets you the brand of tissue or whatever it is you really want. Now tell me, what is important enough that it's worth hurting the person you say you cherish in order to gain it? Let's make a list together."

At that point both parties usually look a little stunned and sheepish. They'd never really thought about it like that. If you truly cherish someone, there really is nothing worth hurting your partner in order to gain. There is no object or point to be made that is more important than the one you pledged to cherish for the rest of your life. Here's a simple truth. If you really love someone, you do everything in your power not to hurt that person. You certainly do your utmost not to become so sloppy in your interactions that you verbally trade punches to the face.

I generally tell the couples that I'm not trying to oversimplify their problems. I realize there are real issues that might stand between them. We can get to those, I tell them, but only if first they can stop hurting each other. There is no way we can find healing and even intimacy if they continue to hurt each other. (Certainly, if they're trying to parent children that need their help, they'll never be much use as parents if they keep hurting each other.)

The homework assignment for the couple is very simple. Until I see them the next time, they are to place "not hurting each other" as their top priority. Regardless of whatever issue comes to the table and needs discussion, if they can't discuss it without hurting each other, they have to drop it until they see me again. For the time between our sessions, they are to avoid hurting each other at all costs.

This is a simple rule, but not necessarily easy to follow. It requires great discipline and focus. It is so easy to slip back into the sloppy bad habits of hurtful volleying back and forth. You'd be amazed at the results when couples are able to successfully complete this simple (but not easy) homework assignment. They return to my office like a different couple. Sometimes they're like that teen convinced of all the bad ways her parents treated her until her antidepressant kicked in. Her list evaporated. When the couples stop hurting each other, a lot of their issues also disappear.

Like I said earlier, I'm not trying to oversimplify relationships. Couples who learn to practice my "anti-sloppiness, no-hurt" rule still need to look further at the underlying issues that probably precipitated the fighting. It's just so important that they avoid hurting each other if they want any hope of getting to the real issues in the relationship.

If parents of depressed teens get sloppy and start hurting each other, they'll greatly diminish their ability to be a healing and helpful presence for their teen and other children. When I felt myself moving toward sloppiness with Patti during our stormy years fighting Tom's depression, I used an image that helped pull me back to reality. I imagined a small ship wrestling for its life against the waves and winds of a terrible storm. It was easy to imagine the storms because we had witnessed several nor'easters while we lived in a small town on the New England coast. In the image, Patti and I were standing on the deck, holding each other around a mast as the seas tossed the ship to and fro. We couldn't stop the storm, but at least we could help each other hold onto the mast and ride out the storm. We had to focus our energy on holding onto each other. One couldn't survive the storm without the other. If one let go, the other couldn't hold onto the mast alone.

Parents please don't fight each other. Take care of each other! Join together in the fight against *it*—the monster, the devastating illness that threatens your child! Taking care of your relationship is so important. Your relationship with one another is one of your most vital assets in the fight.

One of the things that make this fight so difficult is that it seems never ending. The alligators seem to keep crawling out of the lake, one after another. Every day is another replay of the last. The same questions gnaw at your gut. "What kind of day will my child have today? Will he be safe today? Will she have affirming experiences today or more disappointments? What will he be able to handle today? Will we get to do the things the family has planned? What kind of help will he need today? Will some adult call today and say she's gotten into trouble? What will the future be for him? Will there be a future for her? When will things just be okay or 'normal'?"

Some of these questions may occur to most parents once in a while, but to the parents of the depressed teen the questions become an almost-never-ending, nagging reality. Parents fighting together with their teens against depression learn to live almost constantly on their guard, expecting the next bump in the road at any moment. Even when things seem better, there is still that sense of, "but what's next? Can we trust the good stuff to last?"

It was a long time after Tom started down the road to recovery before I could truly relax. I prayed often for God to help with my anxious thoughts about him. I would catch myself watching his face to see if I could catch a glimpse of the storm clouds moving in. If he slept in one day or missed work because he had a cold or flu, my anxiety would spike and I would wonder, "Oh no, is this the beginning of a backslide into more depression?"

If your child is hurt in an accident, or is dealt a blow by a severe acute illness, it can be a very intense and frightening experience. However, in most of those situations, you have the assurance that recovery is right around the corner and that life will return to normal fairly quickly. Parents fighting teen depression don't see changes quite as quickly. For Tom, the worst of it lasted for at least three years. There are many others who have had similar experiences. Teen depression can be more of a chronic condition that wears constantly and can seem never ending.

As I said, this chronic nature of the illness is another reason why it is so important for parents to take care of themselves. Working to not hurt each other is the first part of the care, but that's not enough. Couples and single parents have got to focus some time and energy on their own selves. When you're exhausted from fighting your child's illness, taking care of yourself can seem like another task on a never-ending list. However, please take it seriously. Even though it may require some effort to take care of yourselves, the results are worth it. This is the same point I made before, about playing with the family. It takes effort, but actually restores life energy to an otherwise depleted soul.

Parents need to care for themselves spiritually, emotionally, and physically. Maintaining a healthy spiritual life is vital. That may take many forms, including personal study and prayer as well as participation in a community of faith. Find a community that can embrace some of the spiritual dynamics I mentioned earlier. Stay away from those that don't seem to want to try to understand your struggle. One day Patti and I visited an adult Sunday school class. It was near the beginning of some of the darkest times. Tom had just started on medications. The class began with a couple of members trading "Prozac jokes." Needless to say, we never went back to that class.

Parents also need to play with other adults. Parents need more than just time away from their depressed teen and their other children. They need to engage in activities that give them the opportunity to have fun or provide a sense of accomplishment and fulfillment. Patti and I belonged to a community choir called the New Dominion Choraliers. The choir performed formal concerts as well as miniconcerts in retirement homes, veteran hospitals, community parks, etc. Patti sang alto and I played drums for the group. The choir was a very important part of our self-care during the struggle.

I don't think either of us would have made it through the dark times if we had not had friends we could confide in. Family was helpful, but many miles away. We needed people close by we could vent to on a regular basis. We needed trusted people we could run our thoughts by to determine just how crazy some of our ideas might be. Patti and I needed people who could tell us it was obvious to them that we were doing our best at parenting Tom, especially in the times when our best seemed to result in little or no progress for Tom.

Patti and I also needed people to challenge us. We needed people who would push us to turn the problem of the moment upside down and look at it from another angle. We needed people to help us see our blind spots and confront our own ghosts that might be getting in the way. We needed our friends. We needed friends who could face their own fear of helplessness and walk with us. Fortunately, we found several of those friends.

There are several places in the Gospels where the writers record how Jesus went off by himself to rest or pray. Even in his darkest hour, Jesus excused himself momentarily from his disciples and went to the Garden of Gethsemane to pray. His retreat helped prepare him for the struggle to follow that would show his ultimate love for his people. What better model can we find for self-care? Parents, take care of yourselves. Take the time you need for replenishment of your own souls, so you can "just keep loving" your depressed teen.

7

Spiderman and the Hulk
(A Wedding Dinner with Superheroes)

Celebrating a Miracle

Tom and Monica planned a very simple wedding. They were to be married on the sands of Daytona Beach, Florida, with family members joining them for the ceremony. A celebratory dinner would follow at a nice local restaurant. The two would spend their honeymoon enjoying the thrills of one of their favorite spots, Orlando. Family members actually were invited to ride a few roller coasters with the newlyweds the day after the wedding. How's that for unorthodox?

As details were being finalized, three angry siblings visited Florida, rivaling one another in the amount of havoc created by the destructive path each clawed through the state. Their names were Charley, Frances, and Ivan. As each hurricane made its appearance, we listened to the news and made inquiries about the state of the state. Despite the damages, tourists were encouraged to keep their plans to visit the state. Officials said the tourism dollars would help the state's economy as it recovered from the storms. Plans continued for the wedding to be held September 28 on the white sands of Daytona Beach.

Patti and I were to leave a few days early to finalize some last minute preparations, set up some surprises for the couple, and have a little extra fun of our own. We were going to drive to Daytona, so we could carry a lot of extra goodies for the wedding in our car. As we made preparations for our departure, another storm began to threaten the region. Not to worry! The weather prognosticators said hurricane Jeanne was changing direction, and would steer clear of Florida. Whew!

Patti and I packed the car and headed for Interstate 95 near our home in northern Virginia. As we hit the ramp onto the interstate to begin the journey south to Daytona Beach, we tuned the car radio to pick up the national news. Somehow we really weren't that surprised when we heard the leading story. Well, what do you know? Hurricane Jeanne had changed her mind again. Now she was turning and making a beeline straight for Florida. The rest of the journey with Tom had been an adventure, so why should this part be any different?

At that point, all plane and lodging reservations were made, so all we could do was keep driving toward Daytona and hope for the best. Along the way Patti and I began to think about alternative options if worse came to worst. To be honest, the well of ideas was pretty dry, so we hoped for the best. Maybe Jeanne would change her mind again, and the sunny beaches of Daytona would still host the celebration.

We followed the news of the storm as we headed south. By the time we arrived in Daytona Beach late that night, it appeared pretty certain the storm would pass directly over that part of Florida. The prospects of celebrating a wedding on the beach were looking pretty bleak.

As Patti and I checked into our hotel, we were warned that there might be a mandatory evacuation within 48 hours. I asked the manager and staff if we should turn around and leave the state or go somewhere else inland, like Orlando. Everyone suggested Orlando as the safe place to ride out the storm. "Nothing ever happens to Orlando," seemed to be the shared opinion of the staff and a few other locals we quizzed.

Sure enough, the next afternoon we were ordered to evacuate from Daytona Beach by 6:00 AM the following morning. At 5:00 AM Patti and I headed for Orlando. We found a small motel for the night and began making plans with Tom and Monica to move the whole wedding to Orlando. Rebekah would fly in from her college in Maine. Tom and Monica would fly in from Virginia. The rest of the family members planning to attend the wedding would drive straight to Orlando.

Since the storm was about to hit, there was not much we could do except make our lodging reservations for the rest of the week and enjoy our day at Epcot in Orlando. Patti and I finished the day at the park only to learn that Jeanne had changed her mind yet again. This time she decided to bypass Daytona Beach and head directly for Orlando. Weren't we the lucky ones! The adventure continued . . . .

The power was knocked out sometime early in the storm's sweep over the area. That morning we awoke in the darkness to the howling of category-three-hurricane-force winds. It was a fascinating and humbling experience. We watched all day from the shelter of our tiny motel as the winds tore at the trees and buildings. Debris was flying, and rain was traveling sideways. Roofs and trees left undamaged by the earlier storms were being shredded by Jeanne's ferocious winds.

At one point I couldn't resist the temptation any longer, so I put on my rain parka and headed outside. I wanted to feel what it was like to stand in the midst of such awesome power. The parka was useless. The intensity of the rain drove the droplets right through the parka's guaranteed-water-proof fabric. How amazing and humbling it was to be out in the fury of that storm. (Shhhhh . . . don't tell my mother!)

Hurricane Jeanne ripped across the region, fading by the end of the day. Thankfully, power was quickly restored in our area. The next morning Patti and I scrambled to put a wedding and dinner together. Tom, Monica, and Rebekah were due to fly in the next day. The wedding would follow the day after their arrival. We needed a place for the ceremony, a cake, and a restaurant for the dinner. The clock was ticking. No actually, racing.

Patti and I drove all over Orlando and the surrounding areas to find a suitable place for the wedding. Some of the parks nearby were already booked. Apparently, Orlando has become a very popular location for these occasions. The other available parks were still recovering from hurricane damage and couldn't guarantee they would have enough fallen trees and limbs removed in time to open the park for the wedding. Finally, we found the small state park with a lovely (alligator-infested) lake and stately oak. For some reason it had sustained very little damage. The park rangers readily granted our request to hold the ceremony beside the water. We had the site for the wedding; now all we needed was a place for the dinner and a wedding cake. Whew. One down and two to go!

We practically had to beg a local establishment for a wedding cake. Special orders generally required weeks to process, not two days, the staff told us. We gave them our best sad story about the hurricane and the movement of the wedding to Orlando. Finally, the manager relented, even agreeing to deliver the beautiful cake to the restaurant personally. What restaurant? We still needed a place for the wedding dinner. Two down and one to go!

Patti and I began making inquiries. We wanted an especially nice restaurant, one where the staff would make the young couple feel really special. After all, the fickle-minded Jeanne had smashed their simple but special plans for a wedding on the sands of Daytona Beach.

Finally, someone suggested Emeril's of television fame. We called and found the folks there eager to help us. They understood our dilemma and promised to make it a spectacular event for Tom and Monica. The wedding cake had a place for delivery. Three down! However . . . .

When I asked about the restaurant's location, things began to get a little more interesting. Emeril's is part of the Universal Studios complex in Orlando. The restaurant is located inside the main entrance to the park not far from the Marvel Comics section where Spiderman and the Hulk hang out. What a coincidence! Spiderman and the Hulk chased Dr. Doom and his henchmen around our home on many a day when Tom was a young boy. Now they would be part of another important moment in his life. It was perfect, a wedding dinner with superheroes. Almost . . .

There was a catch. As the restaurant staff gave me directions, I discovered there was no way to drop off the wedding party at the door of the establishment. Emeril's is located in the heart of the Universal complex known as Citywalk. It's like the main street for the entire park, filled with several restaurants, shops, entertainment areas, and a large theater. In order to reach the front door of Emeril's, the wedding party would have to leave their vehicles in the valet parking lot, enter the park gates, and walk down the long main street with all the other park guests. I thought that would be interesting.

The big day quickly arrived. Everyone assembled. The stately oak spread its shade. The alligators remained in hiding, and the wedding was celebrated. It was an incredible moment for us all. Joyous tears were wiped away, pictures taken, and everyone piled in the cars for the trip to Emeril's. We arrived at Universal Studios, gave our cars to the parking valets, and began the walk to the restaurant.

Monica was dressed in a formal long wedding gown, and Tom was decked out in his finery. They were both indescribably beautiful and handsome. *Glowing* is probably the closest I could come to the right word. Walking arm in arm, they slowly strolled down the middle of the crowded Citywalk street. I worked my way over to the side, trying to stay ahead of the happy couple to get more photos and video.

At first the crowd seemed puzzled, taking Tom and Monica for street actors adding to the park's atmosphere. In a flash faster than it takes Spiderman to change into his Spidey duds or the Hulk to transform into his mighty megaself, things began to change. The crowd suddenly realized this was no act, that they were witnessing the real thing. Like the Red Sea parting for the Israelites to walk on dry land, the crowds moved aside and formed a corridor down the middle of the long street for the newlyweds. Applause and cheers erupted. Shouts of, "Congratulations!" and "Way to go!" echoed down the canyon walls of Citywalk. Tom and Monica beamed and continued their slow stroll toward the restaurant.

It's too bad, but the photos and video I took are horrible —it's hard to hold the camera steady when you're sobbing joyously. You see, the crowds thought they were simply cheering for a proud new couple on the first day of their new life together. I knew better. The celebration the crowd was joining involved much, much more than that!

A few days earlier I'd been sorting through some old files and happened across the ominous note from the dark days. (When I reread it, I thought of how Tom had told me he doesn't remember writing it at all.) As the crowds joined the celebration, I couldn't help recalling the words from the note that had once chilled me to the bone, ". . . I would like you to tell everybody I know to tell everyone else I am dead to the world." This crowd of Universal patrons was witnessing and cheering for more than the expression of love between two young people. These folks were party to a resurrection. They were all witnesses to a miracle.

The one who was once "dead to the world" was overflowing with the love of life as he walked beside the love of his life. This was truly a miracle of God's healing, loving Spirit unfolding right before our eyes. The miracle wasn't instantaneous like those recorded in the Gospels but certainly just as dramatic.

The Gospel of John records how Mary and Martha sent word for Jesus to hurry to the aid of their brother Lazarus who was very ill. By the time Jesus arrived, Lazarus had already died and his body was entombed. Jesus directed the people to remove the stone from the entrance and commanded Lazarus to rise from the dead. Lazarus obeyed and returned from death to rejoice with his family and friends. In Orlando, I realized God's miracle had happened again. This time, the hand of God guided Tom, the one who had been "dead to the world," back to the land of the living. What a moment to be part of! What a life to be part of! Thanks be to God!

You can't write an ending for a story that isn't finished, for a life that has a lot more living, so this book has no ending. Instead, it closes with lots of beginnings. Tom and I hope the book provides new beginnings for others who may be walking in darkness and fighting the monsters we have come to know all too well. The healing, loving hand of God can reach forth and call those crippled by this ugly monster of depression to walk again. The God whose love guided Tom back from the dead wants healing for us all.

Teens, if you find yourself walking in the darkness of depression, we hope in reading this you'll find you're not alone. Our thoughts and prayers are with you, as well as those of many others who care about you. Even if you find yourself at a time when it feels like no one really cares, go back and reread Tom's note. He once felt and believed no one cared. Now he knows there were people caring and praying for him all along. He can feel their love once again.

Hopefully, you can believe that as well. There are people who care about you and want to help. Hold that thought until you can feel it in your heart. There is light at the end of the tunnel, and it's not from a speeding train coming to run you over. It's the light of hope. It's the light from the Spirit of God that the people who care about you are carrying to illumine your way. Hold on! The light will get brighter. There is hope for the future.

Parents, if your precious child is fighting this awful monster, then know that our thoughts and prayers are with you as well. We know there will be times when you also need someone else to hold the light for you. Find those people and hold on. They're out there. Take care of yourselves. Your precious child needs you, even when they may be telling you they don't. The light will shine in the darkness. The darkness cannot overcome it. God's miraculous, healing love can work through you and others for your child. Hold on, and "just keep loving them."

Bibliography

Beck, A. T. "The Core Problem in Depression: The Cognitive Triad." In *Depression: Theories and Therapies*, edited by J. H. Masserman, 47–55. New York: Grune and Stratton, 1970.

Einstein, Albert. "Brainy Quotes." No pages. Accessed February 21, 2007. Online: http://www.brainyquote.com/quotes/a/alberteins133991.html.

Lasagna, Louis. "A Modern Hippocratic Oath." No pages. Accessed April 3, 2007. Online: http://www.aapsonline.org/ethics/oaths.htm#lasagna.

Lucas, George. *Star Wars: Episode I The Phantom Menace*. Lucasfilm Ltd & TM, 2001, DVD.

Metallica. "Invisible Kid." On *St. Anger*. Produced by Bob Rock and Metallica. E/M Ventures, 2003, CD.

Nelson, Gary and Bryant Johnson. "A Father's View." On *Take the Call*. Produced by Bryant Johnson and Gary Nelson, self-published, 2004, CD.

Ontario Consultants on Religious Tolerance, "Facts About Suicide." No pages. Accessed February 21, 2007. Online: http://www.religioustolerance.org/sui_fact.htm.